The Rise of an American Cowboy

Published by New World Media
A division of Trident Media Company
801 N Pitt Street, Suite 123
Alexandria, VA 22314 USA

The Rise of an American Cowboy

By Lee, Myung Un (Ph.D.)

About the Author

Dr. Lee, Myung Un is a full professor at Kongju National University (KNU) in Kongju City, ChungNam, of the Republic of Korea.

He was born in 1944, and studied English at KNU (BA), Korea University (M.Ed.), Wayne State University in Michigan (Post-Master), Florida State University (MA), and Jubilee International College in Australia (Doctor of Letters), and Preston University in the United States (Ph. D. in English literature).

Professor Lee has contributed to the Korea Times for over twenty-five years, and runs a research office for world literature.

Dr. Lee has written many books and theses, including *Literature and Life, the Future of Mankind*, and *Cowboy vs. Samurai*, and has translated a Korean novel and poems into English.

He made his debut on the Korean literary stage as a poet. He is also an essayist, and has written many poems, essays, and literary criticism in journals and magazines.

Minerva Press, London, England in 1999, had first

published his biographical novel of the end of the twentieth century, *The Coming End of the USA*. In addition, the same publisher published his second novel, *Night Train-Into or Beyond Darkness*, in 2001.

Contents

CHAPTER 1
A Gloomy Sundown

Toward sundown, clouds were gathering in the sky, and suddenly it looked likely to rain.

I was just arrived home, a little tired from afternoon classes.

My wife, meeting me at the front door, said in a low voice, "There was a call from Seoul just a while ago."

"Who from?" I asked her casually.

"From Mr. A's wife. He died last night."

"What did you say?" I replied stunned.

I could not believe what she'd said, and hardly uttered a word, becoming absent-minded for quite a while.

My memory ran back to a friendly meeting I'd had with him a month ago. Then, when I had met him in his office in Seoul, Mr. A had seemed to be in pretty good health.

At that time, we talked about various things, including the future of the Korean peninsula, and that of the world around the turn of the century.

"Well, I firmly believe China will be split into many a small country as before, and Japan will collapse into the sea in the near future, without fail," Mr. A remarked assuredly. Then he added, "Korea will become larger in territory, and form one of the most important countries on earth in the following century."

"How can we Koreans be an important nation in the near future?" I asked him rather dubiously.

"Well, Korea has gone through countless ordeals and difficulties throughout its long history of five thousand years up to now; but if we Koreans have good-natured hearts, and do our utmost for world peace, we can surely rank among the world's important nations, especially in the Asian region, replacing Japan, I'm sure."

Over cups of coffee, we two talked about the future of the world, especially of America and Japan around the century's end. Then Dr. Kim, one of the visitors at Mr. A's, joined us enthusiastically. He was a university professor in Seoul.

Of late, around the turn of this century, everyone seems to have a deep interest in the prophecies about our world's future, especially the ones made by world-famous predictors such as Nostradamus and Edgar Cayce. It may be because everyone feels ill at ease concerning the days to come.

"I'm wondering why Edgar Cayce once predicted that 'Japan must go into the sea,' in his sleep, using the solemn word of inevitability, 'must'. This is curious, quite unlike his other predictions," I said to Mr. A doubtfully.

Mr. A said in a low voice, "Well, I think it's because the Japanese people have had a kind of national archetypal pattern in their mentality 'to return evil for good' at all times in their long history, and formed numberless bad 'karmas'; and these are said in Buddhism or Hinduism to be the original hidden force or unavoidable 'seed' in the rule of cause and effect in the vast universe, I'm afraid."

With a serious look on his face, Dr. Kim said, "I heard that Edgar Cayce had many predictions based on his dreams while he slept. Many of his predictions were about the future of his own country, that some major parts of the American continent including California, the Southern states, and New York as well, would sink into the ocean around the end of 20th century. Isn't that the case?"

It has become widely known that Cayce could perform the so-called 'life-readings' in his sleep, and could know a person's previous life, and the real cause of unknown, chronic illnesses with ease, healing almost fifteen thousand incurable patients in his lifetime.

"You too can do life-readings, and find out everyone's former life and the hidden cause of his or her chronic, incurable disease, even if they've given up on modern medical science and treatment, can't you?" I said to Mr. A.

"Of course, I can. I can do a life-reading more easily or better with a picture than in person. That's because sometimes guiding spirits interfere with a life-reading, not wanting to let his or her former life be vividly revealed;

but with a picture, there can really be no such hindrance. Actually, by doing a life-reading of Edgar Cayce's picture, I've found out the fact that Cayce had the split soul of a chieftain of the Indian Hawk tribe, named 'Dark Moon' in his deep unconcious," said Mr. A calmly.

"They say that the American cowboy seems to have a strong sense of guilt in the depth of his heart," I said.

"In the past, the American whites mercilessly killed about fifty million native Indians, just as if they had been wild buffaloes in the marshy areas, so that they would build their 'Adam's new paradise' on the new American continent. Well, the whites were all strangers from other lands, but they killed countless Indian natives and robbed them of the vast American continent. They also ill-treated the black people, keeping them cruelly as slaves. It seems to me that most American writers have dealt with this deep-seated sense of guilt as the main motif in their writings, always trying to depict an unrealistic love of friendship between the white and black or colored people," Dr. Kim continued eagerly, "I think this writer's motif of friendly love between the same sex among different colored people has resulted from this deep sense of sin in their hearts, along with another theme cwhich is that of 'escape from father (or home or society)'.. Well, we can easily understand the second motif, as Americans apart from blacks, are all the descendants of pilgrims or emigrants who escaped from their home country in the bygone days."

"Well, Dr. Kim," Mr. A said, "the blacks are all the descendants of African natives sold as slaves in this vast continent by whites. So, the second motif may apply to the blacks also. And by the way, I presume the chronic sense of guilt at the bottom of American hearts, and the vicious archetypal national wish 'to return evil for kindness' in the Japanese unconscious, may be said to be the cause of some famous predictions made by Edgar Cayce; what do you think about it, Dr. Hahn?"

Mr. A looked at me. I looked back at him, and then said slowly, "The Japanese people have made many a mountain of bad karma by returning good with ingratitude throughout their long history. And the American whites have committed countless ills and vices by murdering numberless native American Indians and maltreating the black slaves for so long, so they too have made unpardonable karma, with a deep-felt feeling of guilt in their hearts. And I think, Nostradamus might have foretold the would-be 'natural selection' by the Maker almost around the century's end; He must surely despair of the hopelessness of wicked and arrogant human beings here on earth, as they're getting more wicked and vicious day by day."

Mr. A asserted eagerly, "Well, as a person of psychic ability - that is, 'four-dimensional' power and ability - I can say there are three rules of universe active in the vast eternity: the law of cause and effect - that is, retribution, coexistence and co-prosperity, and non-intervention. Buddha was awakened suddenly after a long spell of painful self-discipline, having found out that 'the law of cause and effect (retribution)' governs this universe. This law of universal retribution has been widely known to be true in the Orient, and turned out to be real in parapsychology or psychic science."

CHAPTER 2
A Nostradamus Reborn

In the middle of the 1970's, Dr. Y first introduced psychic science in Korea. He was a medical doctor and an ex-professor in Seoul. He received a fervent response from people across the country. Then I came to know him personally, as he was living in T city, near my dwelling place; and I was a member of his society of psychic research in Korea.

He often invited a pretty-looking Japanese woman to Korea, a psychic therapist, who had the supernatural ability to diagnose and heal lots of unknown and chronic diseases having no apparent cause.

One day, when I was a graduate at K University in Seoul, I happened to read an introductory book about psychic science translated by Mr. A (by a Japanese author), and I came to know that he was a writer as well as a psychic therapist.

Several years later, I read to my surprise an interesting article about a somewhat strange, and unusual psychical phenomenon involving a young, newly-married couple in a news daily published in Seoul, telling that Mr. A would be a rebirth of Nostradamus. This strange episode was featured in the press on a summer's day in the mid 1980's.

Even now, I remember this strange and unhappy case of a psychic phenomenon which Mr. A experienced in person; and according to him, the new couple had been an Indian father and daughter in their previous lives.

It was in spring early in the 1980's.

Mr. A was on his way back to Korea after successfully finishing some business in Japan, when he happened to meet a newly-married couple in the Narita Airport in Japan. Mr. A was very pleased to see them speaking in Korean proudly among so many Japanese people, not caring about the Japanese at all. So, Mr. A spoke to them, introducing himself as a Korean national; and surprisingly, they recognized him, saying that they had once read one of his psychic books in Seoul in their high school days. The young man said that they had met each other in the States, had finally become man and wife, and were then going on a honeymoon to Seoul, with happy hearts.

But, when Mr. A looked at the bride, he received an ill-omened impression for her in spite of himself. He had an idea that she would meet with an accident, and not live long if left alone or without intervention. Of course, Mr. A could hardly talk about this loudly to her husband, as they were strangers at their first meeting with each other. So he called the young husband to the other side of the hall, and quietly gave him a tip about his wife. He told the young man to come to his office with his wife as soon as possible, since his wife might meet with a unhappy trouble in the days soon to come. But if they came to visit his office, then, he said, he would willingly take measures to prevent the impending disaster. And he added again that if they forgot what he told them, they would later feel bitter regret, with no way or option to make things right. Nevertheless, they did not visit him after that time.

About three years passed from that moment. Mr. A forgot about them. But then one day, unexpectedly, the young man came to see Mr. A in his office located on the slope of S village in central Seoul; Mr. A could recognize the young person at first glance.

Mr. A asked him hurriedly, in spite of himself, "Is your wife still alive?"

He asked this somewhat rude and unsuitable question abruptly; and he felt sorry and very embarrassed about it.

But the young man responded to him quite differently from what he expected; and the moment he heard Mr. A, he began to shed tears.

"My wife is dead. If I had visited you as you advised me to do, she would have not died. My wife wanted to come here to see you, but I was too occupied with my friends and drinking to find time to visit you, to my great regret."

As he said this, tears continued to fall from his eyes. He showed great repentance for his mistake. "I wonder, did she have a traffic accident on the exact one hundredth day after you married?" Mr. A asked.

The young man said, "Yes," opening his eyes wide, and sobbing bitterly, saying that he came to feel even more regret at his past carelessness when he understood that Mr. A had no other course but to announce the result of his spiritual clairvoyance to the young widower. The young man had been the chieftain of a tribe of American Indians. He was called Hawk.

One day, when he was out hunting with his fellow braves, he was caught in a trap he himself had mistakenly set for animals, and the lower half of his body was paralyzed; and then his wife ran away, leaving behind her poor helpless daughter. The chief managed to live alone, leaning on his poor daughter. When she grew up to be a woman, she became a source of support for her father, missing out even on her chance of marriage. She loved her father as if she had been his wife. Naturally she had lots of mental conflicts about her father, so, one moonlit night, she prayed sincerely looking up at the bright moon:

"I was born in this world as a daughter to my father, but if there is any other world, I'd like to be a wife to my father, and make him happy for one hundred days."

As she had wanted so strongly to be her father's wife in her previous life, both she and her husband were born into this world again to be a man and wife. But this young wife had a hidden mental agony in her mind. She felt this modern man was her lost father who had died in her past life as an Indian child, not her husband, and felt full of guilt about having sex with her husband.

"Your dead wife felt a sense of guilt about having sex with you, didn't she?"

"How do you know that?" asked the young man in great surprise. He also added he too had had a sense of guilt about having intercourse with her for the first time one week prior to their wedding day. He said to himself it would be quite natural for them to have sex with each other when they were married in seven days, but he did not feel at ease at all. Most unusually, she was a virgin. His wife too begged him several times, asking, "Could you feel satisfied by only a mental and emotional conjugal life, but without us having sex with each other?"

As she was a devout believer in Christianity, she used to pray earnestly before sleep at night. He tried his utmost to persuade his wife not to have any sense of sin about their sexual life, but this was in vain. Mr. A asked the young man another question.

"Did you meet an Native American Indian woman in the firm you worked for in the States, and feel a strong sexual desire for her?"

The young man said, "Yes," and went red in the face.

Mr. A told him that the Native American Indian woman was a reincarnation of his wife in his previous life, and before long, there would appear a Korean woman who had the same split soul as the Indian woman, and advised him to visit his office along with her this time without fail.

One year then passed.

One day, the young man came to see him with a Korean woman in her thirties, who was already married, and had two children but lived alone apart from her husband.

After exchanging initial greetings, Mr. A realized that she was a well-known painter in Korea. She looked just like a Native American Indian woman, as she had a red complexion and wore bobbed hair. Mr. A believed that the Indian woman who had left the young man in her former life met him again with her unfinished karma in this world.

She said that she was under divorce proceedings with her husband, and after she was divorced from him, she would be ready to go to the United States with the young man to live. She was willing to emigrate to America as the man had been given citizenship.

"If you two marry in the near future, you'll have a daughter. And all the three people in your previous life will be united once again in this life. I give you my best wishes."

The two people went away happily, saying goodbye to Mr. A.

In 1922, T.S.Eliot wrote his lengthy poem, "The Waste Land," and it would be a landmark for New Criticism. It has been said that this well-known poem is concerned with the fall of western civilization, not the physical break-up but the spiritual one-the loss of meaning, and purpose of life itself. The work has been regarded as a poem about the disorientation of modern man, and especially the crack-up of modern civilization.

As might be widely known, Eliot had studied Hinduism and Buddhism deeply, and was attracted to them also, even considering a conversion to Buddhism during the worst days of his life. Here in this poem, Eliot is showing his view of Buddhism concerning life in this world. To Eliot, the balmy spring in April is felt to be the cruelest to him. The lilac is a flower, which stands for reincarnation, and man would be born into this troubled world according to his previous 'memory' (karma) and 'desire' (personal wish). Man does not want to be reborn in this prison-like world, but he must be, as he had created unavoidable karma in his previous living; and so, for Eliot, April, the month of rebirth in this life, was surely the cruelest.

The interesting episode of the newly-married couple

seemed to show the stark law of retribution in the universe.

After reading the strange article in the press, I felt like meeting Mr. A in person as early as I could.

On a cold December day, I was able to meet him, personally in his office. On my first encounter with him, I had the impression of an unusual man with penetrating eyes, but we only had a brief talk about my health because of his busy schedule; he was going to Japan the following morning.

Subsequently, at my third meeting with him, I was able to know my former life, and through his spiritual vision on my 10th wedding anniversary, I learned of the heavy karma imposed upon me.

Since then, I had had lots of talks with him about spiritual phenomena, various life problems, and the future of mankind around the turn of the century.

One night, Mr. A told me about his first mysterious experience in a heartfelt voice. Mr. A was a man of complete solitude. No one cared about him, even his parents, brothers and relatives were an almost unbearable torment to him. When he was young, no girl liked him, and his present wife was the only woman who had ever loved him. For the first time in his life he had found affection.

On his way to a barber's shop on the morning of his wedding day, he heard a faint strange voice, coming from nowhere, saying, "If you marry her, you'll live ten years happily with her, but in ten years, you'll surely go to the world beyond. If you are quite ready, do marry her!"

As predicted by the unknown, strange sound, he lived ten years happily with his wife, despite being poverty-stricken; but he always bore in mind the mysterious, strange voice on his wedding day, and he was mentally quite ready to die.

At last the day came.

One day before, when he was aged forty, he happened to borrow a book, *Life of a Yogi*, written in Japanese. He was lent it by a stranger at a bookshop. He read out through the night, and then came to have a faint idea that Papagi, the former great yogi master in India, had been his master in his previous life.

In the dead of night, he knelt down in earnest prayer for the first time in his life, saying aloud, "Oh! Holy Papagi, you are my great master of former life! I have lived happily ten years with my wife. Even if I die now, I will not feel sorry at all, and I am ready to die as you decree. Of course, I am a bit worried about my poor wife and children and want to live longer if I can, but if this is the Heaven's will, I'll be willing to follow God's order. Please do as you like, caring nothing of my mind."

That night, Mr. A died, and went quietly on his spiritual journey to the next world.

He traveled back to the time in the past when he had been

a rabbi in Israel, two thousand years before he became one of the disciples of St. Papagi, and came to know vividly his own numerous previous lives.

After a while his soul, which had left his physical body, was free for ever, and knew the fact that he could go back to the past or forward to the future freely and at will.

He thanked God for his being free from his body, but at that moment, he heard the faint calling of him from far away, and recognized his wife's sincere voice, calling earnestly to his lost soul.

He passed through the endless swirl of universe, then returned to this world by an unknown force, and now could hear the yells of bean curd dealers passing nearby outside the gate.

It was at this very moment that a bamboo blind suddenly rolled up before his eyes, and there appeared Papagi, surrounded by lots of his disciples. In spite of himself, unconsciously, he made a deep bow to the great master of his former life.

"Hello, A! Do you know who you are?"

"I don't know, sir."

"You are the rebirth of my former beloved pupil, Rahiri Mahasha, along with Nostradamus and other souls. He was born here again as A to do his unfinished duty in his previous living. Moreover, you have to fulfill Heaven's calling to save the unhappy people in the 'Land of Morning

Calm'. You will regain the supernatural power that Rahiri Mahasha had in his former life, and you will save many a person from all kinds of ills and pains, and that is why you had to go through lots of hard ordeals during and after your childhood. So, accordingly, your soul had to be separated from your body completely, in order to know that there exist past, present, and future concurrently in the spiritual world, and if you wish, you'll be at one with the notions of other people at all times.

"You'll be a superman, able to separate your soul from your body freely, and travel into the past or future as you like.

"I give you my best wishes."

"Needless to say, you are to repay others for their kindness with love, and just like the old saying of your country, 'Give one more rice cake to the one you do not like!' you will pay back other's ill will with kindness, and you will always feel easy and comfortable. Many a god will help you in every way, and for you, good things will be good, and bad things good to you also.

"But bear in mind that you should never hurt others by hating them, because all the gods will be moved by your sayings, unlike those of other common ordinary people."

Moreover, the next moment, the bamboo curtain came down, and he heard his wife cry out, "My dear, what's wrong with you? Please come alive!"

Then he finally woke from the 'dream' of death. After he rose from the dead, he found himself completely relieved of chronic diseases --he had six kinds. At the age of forty, he suddenly turned into a psychic superman and miracle worker, no longer an ordinary writer.

After this, he became a mysterious psychic therapist and he cured almost two hundred-forty thousand chronically ill or incurable patients for whom modern medical science and medical treatment were useless.

Every afternoon except Sunday, I would step into the traditional Korean tiled house through the front door, which had a bolt, on the slope of S village in the central Seoul, near the ancient palace of the Yi dynasty in the former Korean kingdom. Here, I usually found myself facing dozens of persons sitting in the sofas in the waiting room, or on benches in the narrow garden. They were quietly waiting for Mr. A to show up before them.

Around two in the afternoon, Mr. A used to appear before them; he almost looked Japanese, rather than Korean, with pale complexion and glasses.

When he sat down on a rug in his office, he called every waiting person by name in turn, and had a serious talk about his problems of every kind. They spoke of health, family problems, job placement, and knotty conflicts with superiors at work, unhappy love affairs, and other life troubles, up to strange, and mysterious phenomena, or illness untreatable by modern medical science. They had mostly chronic, complicated or mysterious problems, including such diseases as cancer, diabetes, mental disease, hyperplasia, or paralysis; they also had other strange and mysterious problems of life, unsolvable by three-dimensional means, but by the so-called 'four-dimensional' measures, that is, the psychic or spiritual approach of life.

Hearing about every person's problem, Mr. A used habitually to fall into an 'empty mind' so that spiritually he could be in the same frame of mind as his 'guest', and then come to know the deep-seated, hidden reason for the person's illness or life problem through Mr. A's occult clairvoyance and psychic research. He was a famous psychic scientist and spiritual healer, widely known in Korea, Japan and Taiwan as well.

He always maintained that all the big problems and incurable diseases, strange or mysterious in some way, came from psychic causes, and would never be solved and cured by contemporary science and medical treatment. Through his spiritual research of the 'empty mind' technique, Mr. A could easily see his visitor's psychic disturbance, caused by his own karma in a former life, and told him the psychic disturbance, or obsession of evil souls, which was the hidden reason why he failed in business ventures or suffered from some strange, incurable disease with no apparent cause.

Mr. A said that he had almost every kind of supernatural power and ability (except teleportation), including telepathy, life-reading through psychic research, free travel to the past or forward in time; also his soul could part freely from his body, and his empty mind could be the same as another's mind (cycle) at all times, and so on.

He once said that he had been born in Seoul as a person of composite souls, including Nostradamus, Rahiri Mahasha, and St. K, the late great prophet in the last era of the Yi dynasty, the former Korean kingdom.

Some believed that St. K once said that around the twentieth century end, a formidable disease would be prevalent to warn all the wicked people. When he would be reborn in Seoul to cure this illness, he would use a Western facility quite differently from its original purpose, and try to do his utmost to merge the Western and Oriental medical science into oneness.

Mr. A said he was officially going by the title of therapist of natural treatment. And he was letting his staff show a videotape to all the visitors waiting for his or her turn in the parlor about his own-invented living water of 'AOM' which vibrated sound for the naturally healthy structure of human body.

He advised every ill patient to drink his 'AOM' sounded water earnestly, which could, he said, drive out all the dirt stored in the depth of the human body. He had invented this vibrated water for improving everyone's physical constitution. 'AOM' vibrated water was easily produced by an 'AOM' vibrating sound recorded on a small cassette tape and played through a small speaker. If any ordinary water was resonated by this 'AOM' vibration, the holy words of Buddha, about three inches high above water, it could become a living water, which could drive out all the dirt and foul elements stored up in the human body.

Almost every person in the waiting room used to say, "This 'AOM' sounded water tastes really fresh; and its taste is surely better than that of any other water."

His natural treatment used to make it a requirement that every person drink the 'AOM' living water at the beginning of treatment; he said repeatedly that it could make a human body cleaner and therefore healthier by drinking it eight cups or so for a day about three months or more.

When a person used to drink it, almost everyone would experience stark symptoms of three kinds without fail: the first one is to be sleepy, the second is to feel itchy, and the third to break wind ceaselessly; these were the stark signs for its effective working in the human body.

Mr. A argued that St. K's prophecy of using a modern piece of equipment as a tool for medical treatment, used differently than its original purpose, seemed to mean a cassette tape recorder, whose use is to record and reproduce a sound, not a medical tool to reproduce the sound of the 'AOM' vibration to change the quality of water.

On a fine autumn day last year, I went up to Seoul to see Mr. A, as I had no class that day. He was in a good mood, and gave me a book of his writing in Japanese, titled *The Future of Japan Viewed by a Physicist*, published by his own small publishing house.

Contrary to the sentiment common among most Korean people, who have had a deep dislike for the Japanese people, he seemed to have a warm-hearted love and affection for the shrewd and egocentric Japanese people. I remember, three or four visitors were sitting in the waiting room at that time; and I expressed a negative view of my own toward the cunning Japanese who have tended to act ungratefully toward their helpers, returning evil for kindness in a kind of national archetypal pattern set deeply in their subconscious.

Then, after hearing out all of my remarks in silence, Mr. A asked me in an earnest voice, "Dr. Hahn, please do not have any prejudice against the Japanese people any more." Then he added, "I've written this book in Japanese with a view to giving a warning to the doomed Japanese nation-before it's too late to escape from the Japanese islands once and for all, just before the terrible disaster that will come around the ill-omened end of this century."

He strongly wanted to get his book published in Japan to let those ungrateful people know about the forthcoming horrible catastrophe. This was the catastrophe predicted by Cayce in the 1930's, concerning the unavoidable sinking of Japanese islands into the sea; he had lived a mysterious life as a sleeping prophet, making countless prophecies about the future of the world and even his own country, the USA.

"The Japanese people should move abroad as soon as they can, and try their utmost to be a help to other nations with their good business ability and skillful handicraft in the days to come," Mr. A argued. After this, he said to me, "Dr. Hahn, please have no more hatred for the Japanese people and try to understand them." He continued, "I'll try to get my book published in Japan to save the people there before the unavoidable disaster happens, as there seems to be no time to lose at all for them now."

However, after that time, in a month or so, when I went up to have a talk with him again, he was in very low spirits and a bad mood. When I asked why, a member of his staff said, "They turned down his offer in Japan."

They rejected his sincere offer of goodwill and they had not recognized his good intention to help the shrewd Japanese people by giving them a warning, and letting them take preventive measures in advance. Then I began to explain the meaning of 'must' in the prediction of Edgar

Cayce. As the Japanese people have returned evil for good throughout their long history, betraying their would-be teachers and friends at all times, and committing all kinds of evils on many innocent nations, their chronic misdeeds have formed a national bad karma a mountain high. Edgar Cayce seemed to have revealed in his sleep the unavoidable destiny of the Japanese people in the near future, with their karma accumulated deep in their unconscious.

Mr. A and I pondered about the strict law of retribution in the vast universe. Heaven seems to ask us to keep on doing well in life, but the world we live in apparently is a place ruled by the cold law of the jungle. The wicked people seem to get along well here, in high spirits; but good people have tended to muddle along through the bitterness of life. In this weary world, few people seem to live good lives, as Heaven would ask us to, I am afraid. Heaven's will and this earthly life seem to be in sharp contrast in their nature.

W.B.Yeats, one of the leading Irish poets of the last century, said that the cycle of human history would be two thousand years in his poem, "The Second Coming." He uses the term 'gyre' which means the numerous great prophets have voiced worry and warning in one voice concerning the era around the turn of twentieth century, saying that this era would be the most crucial time for the survival of the human race on earth.

Most of the Western prophets have appeared to predict the possible termination of the human race around the century's end, but the Oriental ones have tended to show a more positive perspective of human beings after the end of the twentieth century. They wanted to warn us that this era would be one fraught with critical events we could overcome with modesty and a regained naturalness in our minds.

One day in the mid 1990's, Mr. A said he had gone through a mystical experience at the hands of unknown force suddenly at night. He felt an unknown force coming into his body from above, as a fire, and he heard a strange voice from nowhere, saying that all the gods should help Mr. A in every way. The mysterious voice continued, "The life cycles of ongoing human history have lasted six thousand years, and seven cycles have repeated until now, for almost forty-two thousand years in all. For those seven cycles, human souls have transmigrated repeatedly to advance on to a higher level, but in vain. On the contrary, people are getting even more wicked and worse in their personalities."

According to many a prophet in both East and West alike, Heaven may have programmed earth for a grand 'natural selection' at the end of 20th century. It would mean the end of wicked and wretched beings, those almost incorrigible nuisances abandoned by the Maker Himself, in favor of a very few 'persons of seed' for the following century, able to survive the worst ordeal in the 'life cycles'. These few 'chosen persons of seed' would be the people for the following century where a kind of new paradise would come on earth after this century.

As witnessed in the Bible, which says that in six days there will be a happy millennium on earth, there may be an unavoidable era of disaster destined before the seventh day in order for the bright seventh day to happen.

In parapsychology, one day in heaven means one thousand years on earth. It is believed that Adam had lived in the Garden of Eden with Eve about six thousand years (six days in heaven) ago, and the twenty-first century would be a start for the next millennium (the seventh day).

Just as was said by Mr. A, informed as he was by a mysterious spiritual experience, the Bible says the life cycle of human history has been over six days in heaven, that is, six thousand years on earth.

From the Christian point of view, Adam was the first father of the human race, and Jesus might be the second or new Adam.

The American cowboys ruthlessly killed countless number of native Indians so that they could build 'Adam's new paradise' that is, another Eden, on the American continent.

However, since my early childhood, until I was a young man, to most innocent Koreans, the American Yankee or cowboy appeared as a good-natured and kind-hearted 'Uncle Sam'. Anything 'Made in USA' was a product whose quality was the best in the world. Really, to Koreans, we all desired to go to America, a paradise on earth.

The popular image of the good-natured American cowboy, American products and the vast American continent had been always with us in the depth of our Korean hearts, and South Korea was the only country in the world where 'Yankee go home!' had never been heard among Koreans until early in the 1980's.

Now, the memory of American cowboys is slowly recalling my past days, especially when I worked for two years in the Korean army as security on the American troopships during the Vietnam War in the 1960's.

CHAPTER 3
American Troopships

Outside the window of my private office for literary research, it was raining lightly in scattered drops from the sullen sky; clouds were hanging low over the whole town.

My old, two-storied office was standing at the foot of a rocky mountain, rising toward the south, so it was usually sunny, and relatively warm even in the wintry weather.

There was a large and wide picture put in a wooden frame on the wall in the entry hall. On the picture painted in oil colors, the sea was rough, and billowed high; the blue waves were out at sea, undulating wildly into white foams in the wind; a dim and weary light of setting sun was shining through the clouded sky. Over the billowing surf, there was flying a sea gull, lonely, floating in the swirl of chilly wind. In the sloppy sands with the waves beating on the beach, an empty fishing boat was lying at a slant; it looked as if it had been lost at sea, not knowing where to go.

The late autumn weather looked bleak and dismal; and a chilly gust of wind was blowing along the street on and off, which looked almost deserted even during the daytime.

A rare, stray military jeep scudded down the avenue, and the sparse apparition of a passer-by with an umbrella up was visible in the falling rain.

When it rains, I feel kind of blue and desolate, but also become calm and even cool in a subdued mood.

Each time I see the rain falling down silently from the dark sky, it often carries my mind back to those days in my far-off past.

It was a blue Christmas day more than thirty years ago. The weather was bitterly cold just like a wintry day, but it was unlikely to snow as expected by people on every Christmas. It was a black-clouded Christmas day instead of a white one. Dark clouds hung low over the town sullenly in the sky.

Quite unexpectedly, after breakfast, I got a draft-card from an old civil servant of my dwelling village office. Drafted into the Korean army for an almost three year-long-military duty as a Korean youth, I had to go to the military training center for recruits the following morning. In those days, to every Korean young man, the compulsory military service was one of the most difficult 'ridges' to cross over in his whole life-way.

I felt nervous and restless during the whole Christmas day, wrapped in the thought that they enrolled me in an unknown military unit in a day, divorced from the free life of a college student.

I felt tense and lonely all day long. Taken from the free-style college life, I was to go into the unknown world of the military alone, early in the following morning; and I was to do my active military duty for about three years of my golden youth.

I struggled to calm myself down that night. Moreover, I dropped a line to Y, bidding farewell to her, and my heart rendered in half; she was an attractive student, a member of our literary club.

I was wide-awake all night long; I could hardly sleep a wink the whole night through.

When the next day broke at last, I got up to find it had snowed heavily overnight. It was still snowing thick and fast, and deep snow mantled everything. When the cold wind blew chillingly, snowflakes began to flutter in the air.

I left my house hurriedly, but my wrinkle-faced mother followed me to the entrance of my village, and she said sadly, "Go safely, my son!" Tears came to her eyes.

Sorrow choked my voice, but turning away from her, in order not to show her my tears, I said nothing at all, and then plodded down the snow-mantled path silently.

I was walking down past Y's house nearby a movie theater, when I felt painful heart; I felt like calling her out, to say a last goodbye, but the next moment, I gave up, and bade farewell to her silently in my mind.

At an open space downtown in the market, I got together

with other young men. One by one, we rode in a truck, and started for the unknown unit for recruit training. The sky looked dark and sullen, and cold snowflakes flew bitterly in the wind, and began to shower our faces wildly. I felt lonely as if I stood alone in this wide world.

By will power alone, I managed to get through all kinds of difficulties, and after having finished the required army training course for recruits, I rode in a military train at night with other soldiers, and went down to P city, a southernmost port city on the Korean peninsula. Then I deployed at a transportation unit nearby on the seashore.

Nearby the unit, there stood the national cemetery for the dead soldiers of U.N. during the Korean War on the far and wide grass-plot, stretching almost down to the shore. The various colorful national flags flew on the tall poles side by side, fluttering in the wind blowing from the sea. The banners were those of 16 nations, which had dispatched their troops to Korea during the Korean War, following the resolution of the United Nations.

At first, I did my pencil-work duty as a soldier at the company's office; but later, I volunteered to be on duty at the guardhouse. When I came off guard duty, I could sleep soundly; I was sleepy and hungry almost at all times as a young soldier. Luckily, I happened to meet J, one of my schoolmates at the guardhouse. He and I often stood guard together at the nearby posts, facing each other. J was very clever, a sociable guy, and helped me a lot in every difficulty.

We two often went up to the beautiful cemetery park for the fallen U.N. soldiers, resplendent with various colorful flowers in full bloom. I would sit down upon the green park grass, overlooking the blue waves absently striking the shore just below me. I dearly missed my poor mother and little sister at home far-off from me. I sighed also for a pretty girl at college, longing for my past college days. When I first entered college, I had been popular among the college female students. I looked handsome after my father in appearance, I guess, but I was rather quiet and speculative in my nature.

Secretly, I liked Y, and she seemed to like me also. However, I left her even without saying goodbye to her.

When I felt lonely in my military service, I would often look up into the cool autumn sky during my night guard duty. Sometimes, I often heard wild geese honking in the night sky, flying across the chilly sky, now making a V, then going in a single file.

One day, unexpectedly, they told me to transfer to the military pier for security duties at the military intelligence office. From then on, for the next two years, I worked security duties on various foreign ships, largely American ships, including huge troopships, going to and from during the Vietnam War.

Every time there used to be a farewell ceremony on the military pier, a huge, mountain-like American troopship would show up at the deep sea near the sea-wall in the morning; lots of white sea-gulls were seen sitting down upon the sea-bank, with a few flying over the raging billows in the wind or floating on the waves like blossoms.

Some tug boats would carefully bump upon the sides of the huge troopship over and over, with a Korean pilot steering the wheel with care, and finally, the mountain-like ship would come to anchor safely at the pier; ships of the largest class found safe anchorage there. Two American troopships would lie alongside the pier alternatively almost once a month; they used to be in port early in the morning or late at night.

It was on a sultry summer night.

I was just coming off duty, nodding off on a chair in the office of the military intelligence. I felt tired from the duty through the night. As a sergeant of the Korean army, I was one of two head soldiers at the intelligence office, who were in charge of two military security teams on the pier; each security team was composed of ten members, respectively.

All of a sudden, some bustling noise outside the office woke me up. I looked at my wristwatch, and it was almost at four a.m. It was just before dawn and the light was poor; there was yet some time before daybreak.

Outside the window of my office, many military police got together around the front gate of the military pier. At dawn, around five, they expected a train to arrive at the pier with the well-trained soldiers aboard from the unknown training unit on the front line. Already moored at the northern quayside, there was a huge American troopship of imposing air.

Two American troopships, 'Upshur' and 'Geiger', had been on and off the pier in turn at regular intervals; they were used to carry the best, well-trained soldiers of the Korean army and marine corps to the frontlines, and bring battle weary soldiers back home safely, returning from the Vietnamese killing fields. The departing soldiers used to get to the pier by train early at dawn or late at night from a training camp.

That day, as before, troops were to arrive at dawn, and then a hearty send-off ceremony held on the wide field of the pier around nine in the morning.

At last, two MP guards began to open the big front gate of the pier widely, so that the train with soldiers aboard could come into the pier safely.

Before long, a military train arrived, and got through the front gate with the bustling sound full of vital enthusiasm. All the soldiers aboard sang aloud their unit songs, such as 'Tiger', 'White Horse', or 'Blue Dragon'. They waved their hands heartedly toward soldiers on night duty on the pier, and many people watching around the front gate.

I came out of my office, and stood wordlessly, waving my hand to them until the train disappeared into the quay.

Every time there was a farewell or welcoming ceremony on the pier field, we used to be alert and feel strained mentally and physically. Especially, in the case of night duty assignment, with a few exceptions, our commanding officer as well as the master sergeant would often be at home, and so a sergeant of night duty might have been the only soldier in charge of our office, fully responsible for everything on the pier through the night. Military policemen were just the standing guards at limited posts, while my security members were to make frequent patrols around the pier and on the foreign cargo ships with military supplies on board, as well as troopships anchored in the port.

I would usually assign each of my junior soldiers to cargo ships, pier field, or a troopship, just after a day and night of duty shifts. The duty on the troopship was highly difficult and important, and so, experienced soldiers usually deployed on it.

When I first entered a troopship, walking deep inside it, I found it so complicated, just like a maze. It was so confusing for me to get out of it, and so, I tried to find a way out to the front gate with the help of an American sailor, where a fat black security guard was standing on guard. He looked strong like a bear with a gun slung over his shoulder. A Korean MP stood there also on guard, and my man fulfilled his duty aboard the ship, making a free and complete patrol repeatedly.

All the American civilian sailors, including the fat security guard, were very kind to our Korean soldiers, who were off to Vietnam to fight for their lives against the wicked Vietcong and North Vietnamese army, together with the American GI's. They liked the names of Korean military units, such as 'Tiger', 'Blue Dragon', and 'White Horse'.

They said that when they held the very first farewell ceremony on the pier, the Korean president, with the government ministers and many generals, had attended the national event, along with a host of students and citizens, all holding small flags in their hands.

Korean air force planes were flying over the enormous troopship, and just before the ship started to embark for Vietnam, all the soldiers aboard threw out colorful paper tapes, holding the ends in their own hands, and began to sing aloud the brave-hearted songs of their military units, such as 'Tiger Division', and so on. This touched the hearts of everyone there, and many had tears rolling down their cheeks.

At last, the gong for departure sounded, and the

mountainous troopship started to move slowly off, with five-colored tapelines flying freely in the wind like a stream.

Korean army personnel went to Vietnam to fight against the red Vietcong, and they fought so bravely that the Vietnamese people soon knew them as the dreadful 'Daihan', meaning Koreans.

When I was on duty on the troopship, American sailors were friendly and nice to us Koreans, but occasionally, some drunken people would shout, "Go to your monkey cage!"

Sometimes, when I entered a cabin on the troopship or cargo ships, I would find most of the American sailors had papered pictures of naked women or female genitals with pubic hair on the walls, arousing a burning carnal desire in every person who saw them.

As soon as an American ship was moored alongside the pier, all the sailors were busy adorning and shaving themselves, and hurriedly landed at the port, giving off a sharp scent, to meet girls at the 'Texas village', not far from the front gate of the port. They wore broad smiles on their faces, and each sailor carried with him a paper bag with lots of cosmetics, cakes, and a small transistor radio or something like that in it.

They would often talk about girls in their cabins, and wanted strongly to have sex with young women.

Well, strangely, when we were aboard the rolling ship on the open sea, we could hardly control the sexual desire rising within ourselves, and naturally, sailors would have burning carnal desire when aboard a ship.

I made many friends with the Americans and sometimes, some of them asked me to write a letter to his girlfriend in the States for him. One of my close American sailor friends used to show me a picture of young Korean girl every time I met him on his ship, "Hey, soldier, this is my girlfriend, my love."

"Is she your true girlfriend?" I asked him.

"No, she fucks with everyone if he pays," he said calmly.

Early in a morning, I happened to be relaxing in a chair at the front gate of the port, when a sailor ran quickly by the front gate and on to the pier, where his cargo ship stood anchored. Then just after the sly looking sailor went on to the pier, a young woman, who was almost naked, rushed up to catch the escaping person. She said, "That ugly good-for-nothing slept the whole night with me, and ran away when I was asleep, not even paying twenty bucks for my services. A real bastard, I can tell you. Will you please help me get him?"

Along with a Korean MP, I ran after him, and finally caught him just before he got aboard and disappeared into his ship. However, the brazenfaced person just said repeatedly, "Well, I fucked with her last night, but have no money to pay for her at all. I don't know-what do I do now?"

We began to argue with him, and finally, he paid her twenty bucks. She thanked us many times and returned to 'Texas village' with a merry heart.

Whenever I had any spare time during my duty on the ship, I read the novels stocked on shelves in the book corner of the lounge, and some friends gave me one or two English books to read.

For two years, I worked faithfully as a Korean security soldier on foreign ships. These were mostly American, but sometimes, from other nations.

Occasionally, some soldiers complained about Korean people, saying, "Fuck the Koreans! They are all 'slackly boys', you know?"

One day one of junior men asked me, "What in the world does the word 'slackly boy' mean? I do not know what it means at all. So every time American guys call me a slackly boy, I just give them a smile."

One summer night, when a Korean knocked on the door of a cabin of a ship from Alaska, some rough-looking sailors with ugly sword cuts on their faces shouted sharply, "Fuck off, Korean! Get away from here, you son of a bitch!"

Most of the American sailors liked us, and were very

kind-hearted to our people, saying, "We helped you in the Korean War, and now, you are helping us a lot in Vietnam. We are real friends with each other, aren't we?"

Not far from the pier was the notorious 'Texas village', where many clubs had opened for foreign soldiers, mostly for the American crews. Many young girls hung about there to sell themselves for money. The brightly lit clubs in 'Texas' did not want Koreans, and the girls did not like them either, but favored Americans, and were ready to sleep with them to make more money.

One night, I happened to come aboard a ship from Yugoslavia for a cup of coffee. Even though the ship could lie moored in the pier, its crew could not land at the port, as the country was one of the 'unfriendly' nations at that time.

All the sailors, including the captain, stayed helplessly on the ship, and each time they saw me they said in a desperate voice, "Girl, girl, please bring me a girl...!"

As a security soldier, I had to make a patrol around the pier and on the ships moored at sea. There was a ship in from Mexico, I remember. There were two strong youths in a cabin with an open door; but few were on the ship and on a deck on such a fine Sunday afternoon.

"Why don't you go out downtown in this nice weather?" I asked them casually.

They just shrugged their shoulders, saying nothing.

However, the next moment, the two Mexican sailors giggled knowingly behind me. Each time I turned back, they hid something unknown inside their underpants. Soon, I found out that they had been playing with their cocks, hiding them hurriedly whenever I looked back. They were killing the idle time miserably in their room, as they had no money to have fun with young girls located downtown in the port city. A sad story, I thought.

The American cowboys had fought against the aggressive red communists in Korea in the 1950's, and now they were involved in the troublesome Vietnam War to prevent a communist takeover in 1960's.

The Korean government decided to dispatch the well-trained ROK army and marine corps to the Vietnamese 'mess' to beat back the wretched and cunning reds, in close cooperation with the US army. President Park of Korea said, "We Koreans are ready to pay back good for the kindness American cowboys rendered to us during the Korean War."

For two years, I worked as military security in the port city; there had been regular farewell ceremonies for the Korean soldiers who were off to the Vietnamese battlefields as the 'peace-keeping' force in Vietnam, in friendly cooperation with the cowboy soldiers.

In addition, there were regular hearty welcoming ceremonies held for the Korean soldiers coming safely home from Vietnam. All the soldiers looked sun-tanned, and much manlier, like tigers, having fought with fearless bravery against the Vietnamese reds.

In addition, it was on a summer day when I happened to meet her in the pier. She was also attending the send-off ceremony with other people, holding a small flag in her hand.

However, as soon as the ceremony was over, and the troopship was slowly moving off toward Vietnam, it began to pour down from the clouded sky all of a sudden. All the attendants were busy getting away from the sudden rainfall, fleeing back and forth for a safe escape from the downpour.

She was dressed in white, and looked almost like a lily to my eyes at that time; but in a different view, she looked so pretty, giving me kind of impression of cosmos, I could say.

Hurriedly, I fetched an umbrella for her from the nearby building, and led her into my office near the front gate.

"Please sit on this chair and make yourself comfortable, Ms.," I said kindly.

"Thank you very much. It's very nice of you, soldier," said she with a soft voice.

"I'm Sergeant Hahn, and working now for this intelligence office. What brings you here today, if you don't mind?"

"My brother went off to Vietnam just a while ago; he'd

been first in the front line, but volunteered to go to the killing field as one of soldiers of Tiger Division."

"I also tried to go there, but could not, because I'm to be discharged from the army in the following spring. I'm so happy I'll be able to go back home and return to college before long," I said calmly.

Outside the window of my intelligence office, the rain continued to fall down from the clouded sky. She was waiting for the rain to let up for an hour or so. No one was in there but the two of us. On and off, the phone rang while we were talking, but nothing else disturbed us.

"My brother had been also a student before he joined the army. Like you, he is going back to college when he returns from Vietnam safely, I think."

After some mental reservation, she began to introduce herself; she was a female student at K women's university in that port city. She said she was majoring in Korean literature, and her brother majored in law at school, having studied for a national examination.

I made tea for her, and we were talking over a cup of fresh- drawn tea. However, outside the office, it did not seem like the rain would stop at all.

"Well, Mr. Hahn, I guess I must be going now; I stayed here too long, and bothered you too much. The sky is not likely to clear soon. Thank you again for your kindness."

"Not at all, Ms. G., it was my pleasure, and I'm happy to

get to know you like this."

I led her out of the front gate with umbrella up, and tried to get a taxi for her.

Then Mr. Kim, a camera operator working around the front gate, came up to us and said, "Sgt. Hahn, is this your girl friend? She is so pretty, isn't she? Well, let me take a shot of you for free," and then took a picture of us abruptly.

"No, you're so rude and thoughtless, Mr. Kim! She is not my girl friend, you know?" I said quite embarrassed, and then looked at her awkwardly.

"That's alright, Mr. Hahn. Well, I have to get going now, good-bye!"

She smiled and then got into a taxi and left.

When she was gone, I felt a kind of vanity in the depth of my heart unknowingly. She was pretty, and a little pale-faced, I remembered.

As a former college student, I felt warm-hearted toward her at our first meeting. Furthermore, I was a lonely soldier far from my hometown.

While she was sitting in my office, I remembered, she was often looking into the falling rain somewhat blankly. Her brother went off to the Vietnamese killing field on that day as a volunteer aboard Geiger, together with other Tiger soldiers.

In a few days after that, Mr. Kim, the camera operator,

gave me two copies of the picture of her and me. Even though it was a picture taken without posing, she came out well, I thought.

I enclosed a copy of her picture in a brief letter, and mailed it to her department of university. In a few days, I got a thank-you note from her.

From then on, I wrote to her on and off, and she answered me faithfully. In her letter, she said she had a good impression of me at the first glance. It seemed like I had looked rather silent and meditative even to her eyes.

Mostly, we talked in our letters about literature, including the Korean and English literature as well, life affairs, and finally love affairs between a young man and woman.

On a fine Sunday, we promised to meet again in the park near the well-known H beach. I was waiting for the promised day to come, counting the days on my fingers.

On that Sunday afternoon, I went to the park with my heart beating with joy. When I got there, trees were beginning to drop their leaves in the blowing wind from the sea. It was the beginning of fall.

She showed up before me, some minutes late from the expected time; and as before, she was dressed in white and wore black shoes. She looked more beautiful than the last time we had met, and slender as a lily just as before.

"Hi! How're you doing, Ms. G?"

"Pretty good, and how about you, Mr. Hahn?" she said

softly, beaming at me.

"I'm just fine as usual. Well, I am so happy to see you again like this. I've been eagerly waiting for this day to arrive."

"Really, I'm also glad to meet you again. You were so kind to me last time."

"No, frankly, I was so nice talking with you."

A few people strolled around the beach. The sea was getting up, and the billowing surf was relatively high; white foams of waves were out at sea. Countless number of fallen leaves floated loosely on the edge of sea.

Many white sea-gulls were flying freely over the swelling waves. She was so pretty and charming to my eyes; but while talking to me with her low and sweet voice, her eyes seemed far off.

Then in spite of me, a sudden thought flashed across my mind that she looked like a white sea-gull flying over the rising billows-a pretty, free but lonely one.

We two walked about the deserted beach, and went up to the hilltop of park, connected as it was to the seashore with a bridge; they said camellia would bloom all over the isle in the peak of winter.

From then on, I was on a date with her whenever I was off duty. She was a lovely college woman, majoring in Korean literature. I was really attracted to her and was pleased greatly to have met her in my life, especially when

I felt lonesome at heart.

She said she liked Yun, Dong-ju the best of all the Korean poets; the late poet Yun had been an unfortunate youth, who'd lived unknown in his short lifetime, and died unknown at the age of 29 at a prison in Japan under its cruel colonial reign. They said Kierkegaard and Kant had influenced him greatly; and his poetry shows his lonesome world of idealism, searching for a clean-cut and ideal world of eternity, largely based on his religion of Christianity.

I told her I liked Kim, So-wol, the Korean nature poet, and Yun, Dong-ju also. We talked about Hermann Hesse and Rainer Maria Rilke, the German poets of 'white cloud' and 'red rose' respectively. However, of all the poets in the world, I said I loved William Wordsworth, P.B.Shelley, and Lord Byron, the world-renowned English romantic poets. Finally, we came to talk about the impressive movies we had seen. I began to talk to her about my past college days for the first time.

In 1960's, when the Korean economy was getting worse, I had a rather free style and romantic college life with no worries about money, as I was one of the scholarship grantees selected nationwide by H Company in Seoul, a major publisher in Korea. As I entered a national college in K city with the top place, I was really known to, and popular among the girl students. However, I had little time for female students, as I was a quiet and speculative student in worldly matters. In the class, a professor would often say to us, "Go see the movie 'The Brothers were Valiant' in H Movie Theater. The heroine's lips look almost like rose petals covered with dew," or "Don't miss 'Ryan's Daughter' in K movie house. It's very sad, but romantic, though." After class, we used to go to the movies, especially American movies, and I liked Clint Eastwood in romantic Western movies, and Natalie Wood, a shy beautiful girl in 'The Splendor in the Grass'. We all learned to sing the American pop songs, and a male student in my class would sing 'The Green Fields' beautifully when it was his turn to sing.

"Did you happen to see the movie 'The Splendor in the Grass', Ms. G?" I asked, looking her into face.

"Yes, I did. It was one of the most fascinating films. The movie had original screenplay by William Inge, and directed by Elia Kazan. Am I correct, Mr. Hahn?" She looked at me smilingly.

"Yes, you are right. You have a bright memory indeed, Ms. G. Well, I think the director, Elia Kazan, may have deserved the greatest thanks for one of the richest movies in the 1920's from those dazed moviegoers, including me, who rose from their seats to the sound of the end siren of the movie, just after the heartfelt recitation from Wordsworth's 'Ode of Immortality'."

The next moment, Ms. G began to recite the last epilogue of the moving picture, the well-known lines of 'The Splendor in the Grass' of Ode with her sweet voice. She looked romantic and even sentimental to my eyes. We two looked like we were part of that impressive movie and the poetry of W. Wordsworth as if we had been Natalie Wood as a shy beautiful Deanie and Warren Beatty as Bud at that instant.

For the first time in my life, I came to fall deeply in love with her just like Natalie Wood and Warren Beatty in that fascinating film even though they had been newcomers to big parts in a movie.

"I'm going to write a paper for graduation on this 'Ode of Immortality' when I return to college. As you know well, Wordsworth longs for the light which was once around us, lamenting the sullen reality that all is not now as it was in the past..."

To my eyes, she looked pure-hearted just like a shy beautiful Natalie Wood at one moment, but as a white sea-gull at another moment.

When I was off duty and free, I would often have dates with her in the park, at the theater, or near the seashore largely at night.

On a chilly night in that winter, when it was sleeting heavily, she began to weep bitterly on seeing me on the deserted seashore.

"What's up, Ms. G? What's wrong with you now?" asked I in a great surprise.

She did not say anything at all; and she just kept on crying with her face buried in her face.

"Please tell me what happened to you," I asked her repeatedly.

Sobbing bitterly, she confessed, "Mr. Hahn, what shall I do now? My brother lost his life in action last week against the Viet Kong. He was the only light of hope for my mother and me in this wide world..."

"What? Do you really mean that? I am terribly sorry to hear that. I can hardly find the words to express my sympathy with you on the death of your brother," I lamented his death quite sadly.

"My father had died in a battle with the communist guerrillas during the Korean War; we are the family of the war bereaved. In addition, unexpectedly, there came a notice of his death yesterday. Now, my poor mother and I are left alone in this entire world...Mr. Hahn, what should I do now for a living?"

"Ms. G, I'm torn up inside to hear of your sad story. Nevertheless, please have the courage to cope with every difficulty in the days to come. As you know well, you're bright and clever, and if you do your utmost, Heaven will be sure to help you, I think"

"Thanks a lot, Mr. Hahn...My brother was an excellent

student at the college, and prepared diligently for the national exam to be a lawyer. Since he volunteered to go to Vietnam, he'd sent to my family nearly all the paid money he got in Vietnam; he was the head of my family, and we've lived on the money he earned in Vietnam until now," she said in a heart-broken tone.

I felt sorry for her to my very core. Despite myself, I took her by the hand, and then hugged her closely, saying, "Don't lose courage, Ms. G, and I'll be with you at all times. Next year, you'll be able to graduate from college, and be a support of your aged mother, I believe."

She sobbed more bitterly with her head drooped in my arms. After a while, she became silent, and then held up her head toward me slowly; her wet face was wearing a tearful smile for me.

I embraced her tightly once again; and kissed her on the lips for the first time ever.

In the bus back to the pier, I was wondering how I could be a help for that poor and lonely girl. I thought I would be able to return to college in a few months, and finish my BA degree in two years; and after graduation, I could be an English teacher at a secondary school...

I believed I loved her deeply with my heart-felt passion and sympathy for her misfortune at the same time. She was pretty and clever, but lonely and poor also, with no one to rely on in this whole world. I felt like getting married to her, and becoming a torch of light to illumine her way of life in this wild field of battle for existence.

Unknowingly, however, she never let me know of her dwelling place or address. Moreover, we used to part from each other downtown in the port city, and then rode in a bus separately back home and to the pier.

In a few days after I had met her at a seaside house by the snowy night, I mailed a letter to her department, but no reply came. I wrote her repeatedly, asking why she gave me no reply; but no answer arrived at all.

On a clouded, off duty afternoon, I went to her university to see her in person, but could not meet her; and so I managed to meet the chairperson of the Korean Department, wondering what had happened to her. From the aged chairperson, I came to learn of the surprising news quite unexpectedly that she had left school voluntarily about two weeks before without a stark reason.

Ah, my girl, my lonely sea gull, where are you now in this wide world? What happened to you, my dear girl?

With the mailing address I got from the report card on her family kept in the Department office, I made my way to her house on the outskirts of the port city. I finally got to a shabby-looking tiled house on a slope of the hilly uptown area. As expected, the house was deserted, and no one came to the door in answer to my call.

When I asked a passing villager about Ms. G, the middle-aged woman said, "I don't know exactly, but they say, she moved to Seoul last week with her sick mother."

"Does she have any relatives living around here?"

"No, she was just living with her mother and brother; and her brother went off to Vietnam last summer," and then she passed down the road by her house.

She was gone from me just like a passing wind. Why did you leave me even without saying a word? Then, what did my love mean to you? Did it mean nothing to you at all? Ah, you were gone from me even without saying goodbye to me...

On my way back to my barrack, the cold wintry wind was blowing wildly toward me; and the chilly snowflakes were showering my face as if they represented my heart-broken sentiment.

Every day, on and off my duty, I would often stand alone aboard the ship, overlooking the sea wall rising above the seawater before the pier; it was standing there firmly, protecting the pier. Mostly, many sea gulls would sit on the sea-bank, or a few were floating amid the swirl of chilling wind over the wild waves.

After that, time was going by silently just as before, with my mind giving no care, just as the flowing water does, to vanity.

One day, just a month before being discharged from the three year-long military service, I happened to receive an unknown letter with no sender on its envelope. When I opened the letter, I found that it was from her, my unforgettable love. It just said 'From G in Seoul, who loved you dearly' at the end of her letter.

"My dear Mr. Hahn:

First, please forgive me for having left you even without bidding farewell to you.

I am now working for a small private company in Seoul by day, and studying my college work at night concurrently.

Truly, I loved you dearly, but I decided to leave you for the sake of your happiness. Now, I am the head of my family, and have to support my old, sick mother.

As you know well, my father had died in the Korean War for the freedom of our people; and my dear brother died for peacekeeping of Vietnam.

Following my late father and brother, who had sacrificed their noble lives for the freedom and world peace, I am ready to muddle through all kinds of difficulties with courage, and succeed in this wild field of struggle for existence.

Please do not worry about me any longer, Mr. Hahn. I will work hard, and finish my college within this year. I think I will be able to get along well in here just like a white sea-gull as you once called me by the name. It was flying freely amid the cold stream of wintry wind over the raging surf, I remember.

I think I will live along well in Seoul for myself, but never be able to forget you all through my life.

Adieu, Mr. Hahn! You were my eternity.

From G, in Seoul, I loved you dearly."

CHAPTER 4
Remembrance of the Korean War

On my watching the sea gulls floating over the rising waves, they would often remind me of Ms. G, my dear girl, painfully at my heart.

I just wished she might have got along well in this lonely world. Tears would begin to gather to my eyes, missing and worrying about her in spite of myself.

Just two weeks before being discharged from the Korean army, I was sitting on the deck of American troopship, Upshur, looking down over at the sea-bank absently. Unlike before, there were only a few sea gulls on the sea-bank; and a lonesome sea gull was drifting just above the wild sea.

I thought at that moment that the lonely sea gull looked like Ms. G, who would muddle through the troubled life alone in Seoul; and the lonely sea gull recalled her dear face to my mind vividly.

My dear girl was gone from me forever; and she would be floating alone over the rough waves of muddy life, only with her aged and sick mother.

Her sea-bank had been her father and brother in the past; but they had laid down their lives for our freedom and world peace. She had no sea wall to protect her from the wild surf of life. Just as a lonesome sea gull was floating over the sea, so would she be flying over the troubled sea of mundane life by herself, I thought.

However, thinking again, every human being might be a lonely sea gull flying over this troubled life in this prison-like world. In addition, that is why we feel always lonely in our life-way; and the reality of life is often one of solitude in itself.

After the Pacific War had ended between the USA and Japan, the first conflict of the cold war was the Korean War, and the second, the Vietnam War.

My unforgettable love had lost all her sea walls of life in both the Korean War and the Vietnam War. Ah, poor girl, where are you now, my dear love? You are now flying in the cold air of life all alone just like that lonely sea gull over the raging billows. Day in and day out, I was lonely for my girl, overlooking the blue waves helplessly aboard the American ships. As always, the troopship had gone to and returned from Vietnam regularly; and sea gulls were floating over the seawater as usual. Nevertheless, the only thing that changed was the fact that my 'sea-gull' had flown-off from me forever...

On a clouded Sunday afternoon, just a few days before my getting discharged from the army, I decided I would wish my girl well, wish for her happiness in life, and simply go back home safely and return to college again.

Against my sad will to forget her, the lonely face of my dear girl was still floating in the depth of my heart like a sea-gull flying over the water.

I was overlooking the sea, and then in spite of myself, fell into a doze for a second. After I awoke from the doze, unconsciously, as in a dream, my mind was slowly traveling back into the past remembrance of the Korean War in my early childhood, in which my dear girl had lost her first sea wall, her father.

My native place is C city, a lake city, where a blue river is running with lots of lakes and beautiful scenery around it. My father was a good-natured prison officer, and my mother was a bright and strong-willed homemaker. My family lived near the train station in C city; and my mother's maiden house was not far from ours. I liked to go there with my mother, and my maternal grandparents always gave us treats such as fruits, Korean pizza, rice-cakes or candies.

However, quite unexpectedly, on a fine Sunday morning in June 1950, when I turned 7 years old, the Korean War suddenly broke out. The North communist regime launched a surprising attack to the unprepared South, with the full support of the Soviet Union, and Red China.

Before daybreak, my family woke up at the sudden sharp cry of a villager: "The red army is coming from the north. Escape! Escape! Hurry up, all of you!"

My family got up in surprise, and went outside to find an endless procession of retreating Korean army trucks going south.

Hurriedly, my family left home to seek refuge in an unknown southern province before the red army got to my village. They said the communist army would kill all the Korean soldiers, police and prison officers without mercy. The reds thought them their worst enemies, and shot them to death on the spot, on finding them; and at worst, the so-called 'people's army' of North Korea killed every member of the public services and soldiers indiscriminately.

Unfortunately, despite the desperate struggle of my family to escape from the communist grip, wretched young red soldiers on the road going south caught us. The red devil snapped at my father, "You must be a police officer, aren't you?" He then loaded his rifle with a bullet.

Panic-stricken, my father became terribly pale in the face, and betrayed himself badly. At this critical moment, my brave-hearted mother stepped forth toward him, and shouted at the fierce devil, "My husband is a serious consumptive patient. Can you see that on his face? Why is a soldier in the 'people's army' trying to kill innocent people like my family? If you really want to kill him, why don't you shoot me first?"

Taken back by my mother's unexpected courage, the

young red devil broadened his face, and chuckled, "All right. It was a test, you know. I believe you are all fervent comrades of our 'people's army', right? Go free, my good comrades."

My family all had a narrow escape thanks to my mother's brave courage and wits; and we continued to plod down toward an unknown southern province, together with other crowds of refugees, not having the slightest idea where we'd find a place of safety in that far-off strange province.

We walked and walked helplessly towards the south for almost a week, and we heard that vicious red soldiers hid among the unending lines of refugees to avoid the frightening air raids of the American bombers. The red soldiers, they said, turned their uniforms inside out in order to look like ordinary refugees.

To kill the wicked red soldiers, the American planes swooped down over the surprised displaced persons, dropped down huge gasoline drums, and repeatedly made formidable air strikes. Terrible pillars of red fire shot up everywhere. It was nothing but a hell in the real sense of word. Countless people died from gunshots, or burnt to death like horses. All the horror-stricken people screamed out, and dispersed as quickly as they could to be safe from another air strike.

My family too ran away desperately during another

bombing raid like all the other scattered people. We hurried to a nearby hamlet seated at the foot of a mountain as fast as we could. Luckily, my family was able to find some shelter at a kind-hearted farmer's house. He was kind enough to let my family share one of his rooms, and sometimes, he gave us something to eat, such as potatoes, corn, and other foodstuffs he had stored for his family in the winter.

Meanwhile, the red army kept winning overwhelming victories, one after another, against the unprepared Korean army. Soon they had colored the whole map of the Korean peninsula red, except the last two southernmost cities.

For the terrible three-month-long occupation by the red army, the whole Korean land was a real-life inferno of hatred and homicide, where all the crazy-looking red soldiers and village commies ran madly about to capture innocent people such as the land owners, the families of Korean army personnel, police and other public officials, and intellectuals.

Some of the villagers, who were mostly of the lower class and not property owners, turned into red commies. One day, all of a sudden, they began wearing red armbands and rushed about wildly with bloodthirsty expressions in order to arrest the so-called 'reactionaries' and 'exploiting bourgeois class'.

The fierce, malevolent communist elements let all

the captured 'exploiting reactionaries' be tried by an outrageous kangaroo court, usually held in the village's open space; they were killed by the same villagers brutally with bamboo spears or clubs. Well, the reds were vicious and wicked enough to use the underlying grudges and grievances of the lower-class people, that is, proletarians, against the people of property, the bourgeois. The red devils forced all the assembled village people to clap their hands loudly in front of the dead people, and announced that this would be the people's liberation from the 'exploiting reactionary bourgeois'.

Without doubt, the three-month-long communist occupation saw crazed killing and stormy violence and hatred committed by those mad reds. Luckily enough, soon after the Korean War broke out, the UN Security Council called a meeting. They decided that Korea needed the UN allied forces to go to the Korean peninsula to drive out the wicked reds for the last time.

Spearheaded by the USA, the sixteen UN member countries dispatched their forces to save Korea. Both the Korean army and the UN allied forces began to hit back the reds, and General MacArthur's carpet-bombing operation was dramatically conducted by ninety-nine American bombers against the N river shore, then occupied by reds, and annihilated the countless red soldiers almost completely. It was in the sultry summer of 1950. The N river was the last defense line of our united forces against the fierce communist soldiers. Well, this overwhelming victory of UN forces at the N river by the blanket bombing operation came to be the dramatic turning point and change of initiative in the Korean War.

Moreover, quite against everyone's expectation, General MacArthur then waged the surprising and dramatic amphibious assault against the red army position on the Inchon shore in September 1950. Soon they were able to recapture Seoul, the capital city. The red army was in a fine fix. The allied troops kept on fighting off the disheartened reds from the occupied South, and the general's heroic Inchon landing operation turned the demoralized red army into a shaken mouse in a trap.

Finally, soon after the recovery of Seoul by allied troops, my family came to know freedom from the horrible communist grasp, and came to enjoy the value of precious freedom. My family had sheltered themselves in a damp and dark dugout, together with other village refugees, at the shady foot of a mountain.

At first, we had lived together in a warm-hearted farmer's house, but it was far from being a safe place as the village was full of reds, and the air raids became more and more frequent in those days. To escape from the evil clutches of the reds, my father and uncle had hidden themselves in the thick bushes of D mountain, the highest mountain near around C city.

One day, a villager who had gone out of the dugout for water, cried out suddenly, "Come out; come out, every one of you! There are many foreign-looking soldiers on that mountain ridge! They look white or black in appearance."

All the surprised people went outside to find numberless strange-looking soldiers in the wood. They looked very tall and formidable; the dark-skinned soldiers looked very strange and frightening to us.

Every day and night, never-ending lines of army trucks with American troops crammed aboard continued to go up toward the north.

My family was hurrying on the way back home, and all the other displaced people wore broad smiles on their faces after their long silence, and were eagerly returning to their own native places.

On our way back home, we came across countless injured, defeated red soldiers who were walking slowly along with a limp on the muddy road. Our soldiers defeated and captured the wounded reds, and often by the brave village youths.

In almost a week, my family was able to get to C city safely; but at the very night when we returned home in absence of three months, some village red commies rushed to my house at midnight. "Open the door you reactionaries! We know you are all in the house. Hurry up, and open the door!"

There came rough and wicked shouting from the door outside; and some crazed ones gave the door hard kicks repeatedly.

I had fallen asleep after supper, when my mother came into the room and said in a low voice in a great haste, "Wake up, my boy, please hurry up!"

I was frightened out from my sleep, and began to cry out loudly. My mother got my forehead wet with cold water; and then I was relieved of sudden fright.

We went out hurriedly, and hid ourselves into a hole dug in the back yard, holding our breath in the deadly suspense.

The red commies kicked wildly, and finally broke open the door. They ran madly about the house to get my family, saying, "Where lie hidden these damned family of reactionaries? Come out from your lurking place at once! We know all of you are around here now; and we'll shoot you all before going up to the north."

We were nearly at death's door; it seemed like our days were numbered. The wicked red devils went wildly about every nook and corner of the house, but did not find out my family, hidden deeply in the secret underground hiding place at the edge of vegetable garden. The wretched reds tried to get and kill all the families of military and police as well as those of civil officers, and landowners, and then flee to the north before the Korean army and American forces got to our village.

My family narrowly missed death, and we thanked the heaven with our whole hearts.

After the reds fled north, and our troops advanced into my hometown, and peace reigned once again.

Every day, we used to watch GIs passing along the streets aboard trucks, and they often threw chocolates or candies down to the curious-looking kids, standing in the nearby streets.

My elder brother would go out of the house early in the morning, and return home late after dark, with an armful of cornflakes and candies.

Usually, the American soldiers were in trucks, often eating little red apples, and all the kids would shout at them, "Hello, give me candies, okay?"

Sometimes, there would be a sharp outcry from a woman in the village, and the woman often rushed into a strange house in order to hide herself, looking frightened, and afraid of something unknown to the rest of us.

There was a story going around that the American soldiers, white and black alike, would ask every Korean woman they happened to meet on the streets or in the village, "Sibi, sibi, okay? Sibi, sibi, okay?"

I, along with other neighboring kids, went around in the village, shouting at the top of our voices, "Sibi, sibi ok? Sibi, sibi ok?" It was as if it had been a song to sing aloud.

One day, my mother severely scolded me, but I did not know the exact reason why I had been scolded like that. Later on, I grew up to find that the Korean vulgar expression 'sib' means 'to fuck' in English, and it seemed that the strongly-sexed American GIs might have been asking Korean women to fuck with them, and all the frightened women would dash into any house they could find to get away from the GIs. They were also afraid that foreign soldiers could rape them when they ran into them in a lonely place. Korean women placed the greatest importance on abiding by womanly chastity or virginity, according to Confucian values.

At that time, the American soldiers seemed very strong, rich and friendly to the Koreans, especially to us kids. They always looked busy eating candies or chewing something unknown in their mouths. Later, I came to know that they had been chewing gum all the time. Until then, this American 'gum culture' looked like something strange and queer to Korean eyes. It was unknown in Korea.

The endless line of military trucks scudded along the streets toward the north, while adult villagers and kids stood by in the streets and gave them a hearty send-off.

Almost as if it was a daily job to do, we kids went out to the main street in front of the village every morning after our meal, and kept on waving goodbye to the soldiers, shouting hurray for them also.

Then, we all believed a lasting peace had been established in my town, and hoped Korea could be unified in the course of time.

People said our allied forces won battle after battle, and marched on carrying everything before them. Soon after they recaptured the capital city of Seoul, united soldiers swept away everything and then captured the red capital, Pyongyang in North Korea, and kept on going on to the northernmost provinces.

Finally, before winter came, our united army got to the Yalu River, which runs across the northern edge of the Korean peninsula. The soldiers drank the river water out of sheer joy, shouting cheers in the hope for the forthcoming unification of Korea.

MacArthur was a very proud and heroic general, and he supposedly compared himself with Alexander the Great in his lifetime. He was convinced he could unify the Korean peninsula for the last time and did his utmost toward this, supporting the proposed bombing of Manchuria, the land of Red Chinese occupation, if it was unavoidable. Well, he was the national hero of the Korean people at that time, and his statue stands even now in Inchon, recalling his heroic landing operation.

The general once said there was only a small likelihood of Red China intervening in the Korean War; but when Red China meddled in the war, he said he would make comprehensive bombing raids on Manchuria to beat off the reds.

However, contrary to his expectation, China invaded abruptly in the bitter cold weather of 1951. The Chinese reds used the strategy of throwing waves of men into action, wielding wildly the 'human sea' tactics. Now I still remember clearly that the Chinese red soldiers had few weapons, with two stick-like hand grenades at their waists, and only a few shouldered long old-fashioned rifles, and that was all.

Struck by an overwhelming number of Chinese soldiers, the united forces had to withdraw unwillingly from the north toward the south; and once again, the South fell into the wretched hands of the red army.

My family had to walk back down to the south, seeking a refuge in a strange place again. We plodded along the way down toward the southern provinces, with other refugees.

On our way going down south, our folks happened to meet a farmer's family from the same village in my hometown; the farmer had his wife, two grown-up daughters and his son's couple.

When the sun began to sink below the horizon, we two families groped for an emptied house to stay overnight. Then my mother said abruptly, "As we have only a light summer quilt with us, how about taking a warm bed quilt instead at a deserted house around here?"

My father said, "No, we must not. We're to live honestly even during the war, I think."

Following her husband silently, my mother gave up, and we all tried to find an empty house for a night's stay. Finally, we entered a deserted house near the main street, and desired to stay in there overnight.

As my father was a prison-officer, we asked the farmer's family in our company to stay in the wider living room, so that we might be able to stay in a more secluded reception room, attached at the backside of the house. We thought it might have been safer for our family and the farmer's family could then stay over night in a wider room instead.

Nevertheless, the stubborn farmer insisted on their staying at the secluded guest room, and so my family members were to stay at the living room, which could be vulnerable to any passing communist soldiers or elements.

In the dead of night, unexpectedly, a passing American plane was flying over the lonely house like a swallow, strafing machine-gun bullets in torrent. It seemed like the

American plane happened to find a red soldier in front of the house with something to eat.

Suddenly, there came sharp outburst of wild cries from the next room where the farmer's folks were staying together. My family, struck with terrible panic, pulled a bed quilt over our heads helplessly in the midst of complete confusion; and that was the only thing we could do at that panic-stricken situation.

Frightening wild shots of machine-gun fire riddled the walls and ceiling; but when the American airplane flew off at last, we found unbelievably that our folks were all safe. We thought that heaven helped us out unhurt.

However, at the next moment, I found that my mother's face was bleeding. Unbelievably, there was a slight line of blood bleeding along her forehead, possibly made by a passing machine-gun bullet.

"Does it hurt you badly, my dear?" asked my father worriedly.

"No, not so much," replied my mother.

"Don't say again to get a thing like quilt at a deserted house."

"I'll never do that again; I think I've been surely warned by heaven for that," said my mother.

"However cold we may be in this winter, we'll not take along other people's thing with us even in the war-time. Do you understand me?"

"Yes, I know what you mean, honey."

Once again, there arose a wild roar of wails in the room next to ours. My father went out hurriedly to see what had happened in there.

Soon he was back to us with a frightened face, and uttered in a great hurry, "This is really terrible. Two daughters were killed on the spot, and his wife was seriously wounded, to our great regret."

When the day broke, my father and grandfather helped the poor farmer bury the dead girls hurriedly at the foot of nearby mountain. Without saying thank-you, the queer-looking farmer continued to blame my family for his terrible misfortune, saying, "It's because of your family. If you had stayed last night at the guest room instead of my family, my two daughters would not have been killed like that, I'm sure." He was crying wildly, squatting down in the dirt like a crazy person.

We had to part from the poor farmer hurriedly, and continued to go south; my family kept on walking down southward for nearly a day month, muddling through all kinds of difficulties with a will to survive.

Finally, we got to J city, and found there countless number of helpless refugees squatting down in the dirt around the wide square in front of the railway station. They all looked dead tired, and absent-minded, not knowing what to do in an unknown place; and some of them almost starved to death.

At the very moment, an American military jeep came slowly into the open square. It stopped for an instant, and unexpectedly, an officer put down a big can on the ground, and then ran off northward. Everyone's eyes focused upon the delicious-looking can, but no one dared to run out in front to get it, despite their strong inner desire. Then, bravely, I stood up, dashed forward to get the can, and returned with it. All of my family members looked very delighted, and wore broad smiles on their faces. Happily, there were many sliced meats with delicious juice in it. Each of us had a taste of the meat one after another in turn, and my grandfather praised me a lot for my active deed saying, "You did well, my boy."

These days, I never pass the square in J city without recalling the big meat can more than forty years ago, and miss my grandfather, who looked so stern, but was kind-hearted toward me at all times.

Then, my family decided to go farther to the city of K, my present dwelling city, a basin-like hilly place with lots of historical remains around it.

We walked on and on for a whole day, eating nothing at all; we were deadly thirsty and extremely tired. However, the sky was blazing red at sundown as usual; slowly, night began to fall thick and fast.

My family pined strongly to eat well and sleep soundly

at night. My father went up to a big tile-roofed house in a small village seated at a nearby reservoir. Following my father, our other folks also entered the wealthy-looking house.

The generous-looking property owner let my family stay at his house that night and stuff our bellies, kindly enough. We almost starved to death, and we felt we could eat a horse. I too had enough, until my stomach was full.

"How famished you must have been to eat like that. Please eat as much as you can, and then sleep soundly on the warm-heated On-dol room," said the property owner in his kind way.

We all greedily ate, and fell into a deep sleep for the first time after we had left our home. It was a sound sleep after a long absence of such rest. I felt lightsome and nimble when I woke up early in the following morning.

After we had a large breakfast, we all took a long rest on the wide and cozy living room, eating some fruits and rice-cakes.

Moreover, the next moment, the kind property owner and his wife were coming up to us, wearing a soft smile on their faces; his wife, I felt, gave me a glance frequently, and the property owner beamed at me also.

I did not know the reason, but was just sitting there, listening to what they were talking about with my parents. Surprisingly, the property owner began to utter a thing we had never dreamed of before.

"Well, I can hardly imagine what you think of me, if I utter this thing vital to my family blood-line like this...but with courage, I'm going to confess what I have in mind frankly. Please give that boy sitting over there to my family. We would like to adopt him as our foster-child. We have plenty of properties, including real estates such as fields and mountains, but have no child to carry on the family line, to our great regret. If you let him succeed to my house, we will feed and raise him well and rich, I promise you like this.... What do you think of my idea?"

"You mean, our second child over there? No, we will never let that happen! He is the brightest child of my kids. However hard and thorny the life-way may be in this war-time, we can hardly give up our children in the world, and never can our second child especially," cried out my mother.

"Don't be so upset, and try to calm yourself down. Please think deeply about what I said just a while ago, and make a wise choice. You are a displaced family, and have three kids to foster, far-off from your hometown. How can you all be getting along in this strange place during the war? Please give that boy to us, and I am going to bring him up well and right, and then let him get on the world after he is educated well. We'll never disappoint you, and I promise you again," said the property owner heartedly.

"Well, don't say such a thing to us again. We will live together, or starve to death together if we have nothing to eat. Nevertheless, we will never abandon our kids in the world. Thank you so much for your kindness. It was very nice of you to treat my family with such generosity; we will never be able to forget you. Well, we must get going now. Take a good care and goodbye!" saying like this, my father rose from his seat.

We were off on our way again; the rich man and wife stood in front of their gate, looking over at me absent-mindedly. I was just going off, waving several times to them, out of sheer courtesy.

Luckily, my father could work for the prison in T city as an officer as before; but the rest of my family moved to K city, our present dwelling place, located by the flowing K river; it is a small basin-like city surrounded by mountains.

For a week or so, we stayed at a temporary asylum, and then moved to a rented house with two rooms and a kitchen in the suburbs of city. Then everyday life seemed a matter of life and death, and we almost starved; we could find nothing to eat, and even with money, we could hardly buy any food.

My mother and I went to the city office every morning to see if we could get some relief supplies; we would wait in vain all day long, and return empty-handed after dark.

Meanwhile, just before my family moved to K city, they said, the allied troops began to advance northward again.

At that time, the US bombers and ladder-like Australian planes made endless strikes on the red army, day and night. I remember the Chinese soldiers we met before coming down to K city once confessed they were greatly afraid of air raids and black soldiers. They often said, "The Blacks are coming. They look formidable at night; we are scared of them really. We are frightened by the bombing too. Well, we do not know when we shall die. The American planes fly over us twenty-four hours a day. We've been thrown into a real hell...we are damned now."

The united forces proceeded northward, and soon recovered Seoul again, and kept on going up the country, beating back the depressed Chinese reds in one battle after another.

During the wartime, we kids saw the American soldiers shaving themselves in a trench, and some of them would run into a river or a deep lake to bathe or swim. My village kids and I once saw some American soldiers attacked suddenly by communists with rifles when swimming in a lake not far from my village. Some were killed on the spot, and others fled away naked in the hot sunshine.

About three years, after the Korean War broke out, in the summer of 1953, both parties-the US, representing the UN allied forces, and the North Korean communist regime-concluded an armistice with each other, having established a new 'Armistice Line' instead of the former 38th Parallel Line across the Korean peninsula.

The ceasefire really went contrary to the heartfelt expectations of all the Korean people, who keenly hoped that Korea would be one unified country after the end of the war.

So, why not a unified Korea, and why has it remained divided for about half a century, as it was before the Korean War?

We still remember that the bright and proud, somewhat romantic-looking war hero, Douglas Macarthur, once maintained he would be prepared to bomb over Manchuria, if it was unavoidable. If MacArthur had been the supreme commanding general of the UN allied forces until the end of Korean War, and not fired abruptly by the weak-hearted president, the Korean peninsula would have unified into one country. Nevertheless, Mr. Truman was worried only about the possible outbreak of a Third World War. He should have let his general act freely in the war. But the US, which had the most powerful national strength around the world, seemed to want to avoid war, unlike the character of its trigger-happy cowboys; it only took care not to provoke Red China and the Soviet Union.

For that reason, the late communist leader, Mao Tse-tung ridiculed the US as a paper tiger. Thereafter, the American cowboys had to withdraw ignominiously from Vietnam in the 1970's. This was the first major defeat for the young republic ever since it had gained political independence from England. They made a chronic mess called the 'Vietnam syndrome', which has led to a crisis of confidence in Americanism, and in the cowboy himself.

In the sixties, American cowboys participated in the Vietnam War, and then withdrew in the seventies, defeated by the poorly armed Vietcong and the North Vietnamese army.

What is the reason why the cowboys lost to one of the most primitive armies on earth? I believe the precise reason may be in the mental attitude of the American cowboys toward fighting a war.

The ultimate purpose of war lies in a victory, and to achieve that goal, there must be the successful strategy, well-trained soldiers, and good weapons and supplies; a firm will to win against the enemy should be the first priority.

While the US was conducting the Vietnam War, some Americans launched an anti-war campaign within the United States, and the government conducted limited bombing of Northern Vietnam, afraid of the possible intervention of the Red Chinese army in the war as had happened in the Korean War in the 1950's. In the States, the war divided and tore asunder national opinion; the troops fought unwillingly, together with the helpless and corrupt South Vietnamese government, against the cunning and vicious Vietcong guerrillas, with no firm fighting spirit, no mental will to win; they just wanted to preserve the status quo. In addition, this resulted in the sad withdrawal from Vietnam.

Now, it seems to me that the cowboys fought against the reds with the same low-spirited mentality in both Korea and Vietnam, and naturally, they had little or no results at all, despite the enormous loss of money, weapons and labor.

That excellent war hero, General Douglas MacArthur, made his famous farewell address to Congress, and disappeared from the stage of life as a soldier. It may be that he was a true soldier of courage and personal pride, and the greatest that the American cowboys have ever had in their national history.

CHAPTER 5
The Cowboy Country

After my military active duty, which lasted three years, I became a college student again.

At the first class meeting, Prof. P said in the class, "Mr. Hahn entered this university in first place; he is the brightest student, I can tell you."

From that day on, the girls in the class began to take a deep interest in me. I was thin in appearance and rather quiet, but read many English novels after school. Encouraged by an English majoring soldier during my military duty, I had tried to read English novels on board ships. Of them all, Pearl Buck's *The Good Earth* and W. Somerset Maugham's *Of Human Bondage* were most interesting to me at that time.

In the fall, when I was a junior, I started to contribute to an English daily newspaper published in Seoul, and from that time on, I contributed to the English press and other journals too.

After I had graduated from university, I became an English teacher at a middle school in a remote hilly rural district, where the deep and fast-flowing N river ran.

The village where my school stood looked like an island around which the N river ran fast through some rocks.

After class, I used to sit on a bench in the back yard of school, and from there, I often looked down at my leisure over the cool, noisy waters of the river.

After two years, I moved to another school near my home, and as I had hoped before, entered a graduate school in Seoul, majoring in English. I was very busy teaching at school by day, and studying for my graduate work at night.

Around the middle of 1970's, I met a pretty-looking woman teacher at a cozy tearoom, via an intermediary, and she has been my wife for over twenty years. She is kind-hearted and wise, helping me a lot in everything.

After I had finished my MA degree, I decided to go to America for further study as soon as possible.

At last, the day arrived in the summer of 1980.

On a sunny summer day, I was aboard a KAL jet at Kimpo International Airport in Seoul, and took a transpacific flight with some expectation and anxiety about my unknown future to come in the vast continent of the USA.

The KAL airplane continued to fly over the endless cloudy sky for over thirteen hours; we then landed in Hawaii Airport and obtained an entry permit. After the required procedure, we flew for five more hours to LA.

From my seat, through the window, I looked down over the apparently endless and dazzling night view of Los Angeles. My heart was beating wildly, and I wondered how I could get through my graduate studies in this vast, unknown country, competing with native speakers.

Having landed at LA Airport, I had to go farther on to Detroit on a domestic flight. I had no time to lose at all, and hurried to transfer to the domestic air service in the over-crowded airport.

"How can I go to the American Air Lines counter, sir?" I asked some passing Oriental people, including Koreans hurriedly; but they just passed me by, saying nothing, or "I'm not going there."

Hearing me asking a police officer, an elderly white man was kind enough to take me to AAL in person, and said with a smile, "Have a nice trip," and then he went on his way. His kindness impressed me, a lonely young foreigner, in that crowded airport.

I got on board an AAL flight at 11 p.m., and would get to the Detroit Metropolitan Airport at seven the following morning.

Two Korean students met me at the airport, and kindly gave me a ride to an old-looking apartment opposite W university, where I was due to share an apartment room with a young Korean man.

After lots of mistakes and difficulties, I managed to study at the Department of English with the status of post-master.

Today, I remember vividly the utter frustration I felt at

the first class meeting of the English graduate course as a foreigner among so many native speakers. I could hardly understand what the young professor said during this first meeting; he spoke rapidly like a machine-gunner, especially when joking casually with the American students in the class.

Lying on my lonely bed later in the apartment room, I was in a serious mental mood; I felt I was fighting with my back to the sea. I had my wife and two kids back in my home country, and they laid me off as a teacher before coming to the States.

Having no one to rely on in this strange, vast foreign country, I had to muddle through every difficulty by my will and efforts.

Early every morning, I jogged through downtown Detroit, and every American, white or black alike, looked at me, an Asian man with a yellow complexion, with some curiosity. After jogging, I used to feel refreshed and strong-willed. Then I went to the State Building, which contained the English Department, to listen to lectures with the mind of a warrior in battle.

As I was the only Oriental student out of all the students majoring in English, all the American students would stare at me curiously, and even the professor seemed to have very little confidence in my ability to keep up with his class.

I tried to listen with my ears pricked to what professors said in every class, but could not catch even half of the lectures. I had to guess the rough contents of each class, and read books hardest, always trying to do my preparation and reviews faithfully as I had done in Korea before.

On a fine autumn day, Dr. C, a young professor, gave us a test unexpectedly in his class, which they called a 'pop test', or 'quiz' among themselves. The American students seemed to know of the test beforehand in the previous class, but I was completely ignorant of it. However, as I had made a faithful review of every lesson every day, I had little difficulty in the surprise test, and got an A-. I did my utmost to catch up with my classmates, and soon the professor seemed to recognize my efforts and my potential ability.

Detroit seemed very dangerous, especially at night. Bullet holes riddled almost every shop window, and some Korean students said that one night they had been frightened out of their minds by a few rough black people on the street not far from the university.

A timid-looking Korean student who lived at the same apartment block on the third floor came down to my room one night, and asked to stay with us, saying he would feel terrified by the dreadful sound of sporadic rifle fire, which we could hear from the nearby downtown streets.

He said fearfully, "I'm almost scared to death, and feel

as if stray bullets might fly into my room. Please, let me stay in your room. Together, we can rely on each other."

This spineless and timid fellow became a nuisance to me for several months.

Every morning, when I was exercising at 'tae kwon do', the Korean art of self-defense, outside the apartment, passing blacks would ask me, "Do you know Bruce Lee? I like him so much. You know, I'd like to learn karate, too."

The blacks seemed to think all the Oriental people have black belts in karate, as Bruce Lee did; indeed, they were afraid of the Oriental martial arts.

I had no car, so transportation was the one of my most serious problems. Sometimes, I picked up a ride by a fellow Korean and went out on Sunday to a Korean church in the suburbs of Detroit. The white people seemed to work in the central city, and live out in the suburbs with their families. Their houses were set among green grass, and looked nice and rather picturesque. The sky was wide and blue, and a soft breeze blew quietly. Unlike downtown, the suburban scenery looked like a postcard heaven to me at least at that time.

Having no car of my own and no time to spare, I just walked back and forth to the university, getting myself absorbed in my studies. On and off, I would attend a class in 'film review' in the university's little theater, and films were discussed by the professor and students alike, after they were shown on the screen; and interestingly, naked women appeared in them frequently, revealing their private parts with pubic hairs clearly, which would not be allowed in Korean movies at all.

After some thought, I thought a good way to solve the transportation problem was to ride in a bus. However, Korean students were afraid of buses, as buses had dark windows and many black heads were usually in them seen from the outside. One day, with great courage, I jumped on a bus at a bus stop in front of my apartment, put coins into the fare box standing beside the driver's seat, and then sat on a seat. Looking around at passengers in the bus, I felt relieved to find them kind-hearted, and they gave me a gentle smile. Downtown in the city, I bought a small Kodak camera, and went around, looking here and there. I happened to enter a shop, and found it was an 'adult shop'.

There were many adult magazines displayed on the stand-sex magazines, showing vividly female and male genital organs, and odd strange-looking sexual positions. One person in the shop said, "This girl is eating a banana now," pointing to a girl having oral sex with a male.

To my surprise, there were many artificial 'portable pussies' and 'portable penises' of various different sizes for sale on the wall stand, near which a young woman was sitting as a shop girl. Then a thought came to me that America was a free country, especially a sexually free country, as I had heard at home.

From then on, I used to ride on a bus freely with no worries at all, and went around lots of places I wanted to see. Every time Korean students met me, they would often ask me, "Were you okay in the black bus, no problem at all?"

My young roommate often asked me, "Is the bus really all right? How much is the fare?" He showed a keen interest in using the bus, as transportation was a common problem among foreign students. However, every time I told him to get on a city bus, he would not ride out of sheer fear and stayed alone in his apartment.

On a fine autumn Sunday afternoon, I went out to a neighboring park, within an hour's distance by bus-ride to the west. I strolled around there, and found many adult movie houses scattered here and there among the houses nearby; and I decided to watch an adult film out of sheer curiosity. The entrance fee was five bucks, and there was a welcoming notice posted, 'Ladies welcome! Ladies are free'. However, there were no women, only males-mostly older people-in the dark theater. Various interesting sex films ran continuously on a wide screen. They were very realistic and lasting about four hours in all. Most of customers, who were mainly white-haired old men, committed self-abuse in the dark. Suddenly, I felt sadness in my mind for them, and recalled a phrase about the misery of desire in W. Somerset Maugham's famous short story, *Rain*. He looks down, like a god in the sky, upon the helpless American sailors in the rain, roving about in the red-light district for desire at night on an isolated island in the Pacific Ocean.

Suddenly the movie stopped, and two young girls, one white and one black, showed up on the stage in the front, began to strip naked, and then went through various naked obscene postures before the customers. After some time, they came down from the stage among the customers, and put their private parts close up before everyone's faces in turn. Some people smelled them, and gave them a generous tip.

Strangely, in that obscene sex movie, young and fresh-looking girls acted as sex partners with the men, including different social strata of males. They were not the worn-out, filthy-looking street girls, contrary to my first expectation.

Well, frankly, we human beings are somewhat dirty in our nature in a sense, when we throw off the mask of politeness; there lays a deep-seated animalism, including the strong sexual instinct. Called 'libido' by Freud, it may be the original inherent force behind human action lying at the bottom of every person's unconscious mind. Some have said that man is the lord of creation, or the noblest being God had ever made.

However, in a sense, man seems to be the most cunning, wicked creature on earth. Other animals act on instinct, but do not wear a wicked mask of hypocrisy.

While Freud emphasizes the importance of sexuality as the essential force in human activity in daily life, Nietzsche maintains the will to power as the original force in the human heart. The disciple of Freud, Adler actively took up this idea, refusing to accept his master's theory of sexuality as the inherent hidden force behind all human action.

Whenever I used to go to the downtown Detroit, I always felt rather bleak in spite of myself. There were numerous bunt-down ruined buildings scattered around the heart of city, looking like damage from an air strike.

There were many alcoholics around the inner city blocks, lying down in the streets or sauntering about sluggishly like human jetsam with bloodshot eyes.

As Dr. P said before, every American big city appeared almost dark under the bright downtown street lamps. At night, as in other big cities, Detroit seemed crowded with black people, as white people would go out to the suburbs after work.

After dark, I used to stay at my apartment room, not venturing out to the university library, even though it was a very short distance. However, my young roommate used to go to the school library every night, and returned to the apartment with some courage at midnight. He would say, "I have no one to fear, because Jesus Christ is always with me." However, I wondered why he was too frightened to get on a city bus even though he wanted to.

One day, during a nice spell of autumn weather, I visited the magnificent Renaissance Center with Dr. P. He had come to Detroit as a visiting professor at D university. The wonderful and grandiose Center stands by the River of Detroit, which divides the US and Canada, forming the border between the two neighboring countries. The Center contains the seventy-three story Plaza Hotel, the highest hotel in the world, and includes four other buildings around it. It cost me just a dollar to go up to the observation floor by a slowly moving elevator, but the elevator was made of transparent glass.

What a thrilling sight it would be to climb up to the top by the transparent elevator! Every person looked terrified, and the thrill and tension was extreme. A young boy and girl hugged each other, chanting some unknown song, and said," Please look up, not down below, my dear!"

The elevator was too slow when it went upward; it seemed as if it was moving forever. Then everyone seemed to escape eagerly from the unease and tension a.s.a.p. Yet the moment we set foot on the top floor, we felt dizzy all of a sudden. Asked why, an American tourist told us that the design of the top floor allowed it to move around slowly, giving a surprising excitement and pleasure to the visitors.

From the observation floor, I looked over the endlessly unfolding land of Canada to the horizon. The Detroit River was flowing along quite leisurely, with the water glittering in the bright sunbeams.

Many tourists were relaxing on the top floor of the hotel. They seemed to enjoy the thrilling tension of the moving floor, and the wide-open scenery stretched endlessly below before their eyes.

A week later, after my thrilling visit to the Renaissance Center, Dr. P and I went to Chicago by train. His wife was due in at the airport early the following morning, along with some other Korean tourists. We were on the Amtrak train for five hours and arrived in Chicago late at midnight, and then checked in at the YMCA hotel. Well, Chicago looked like the gangster city Carl Sandburg describes in his powerful poem, "Chicago", and seemed almost dark like Detroit, though with the bright streetlights.

I was wondering deeply in my mind why most American cities seemed so dangerous and threatening especially at night and the police did not maintain basic public peace and security. I said to myself, "Is this the reality of the world's No. 1 country we Koreans had dreamed about?

Is this the intended 'Adam's new paradise' the white pilgrims had tried to build on this continent?"

From the top of the YMCA hotel, I saw countless gloomy-looking tall buildings rising up through the night mist. It was a wild, strong city with big shoulders. In a sense, it was a city of violence, power and ambition, that is, a typical American city, as Walt Whitman loudly proclaims in his *Leaves of Grass.*

As the plane's arrival delayed, we had some time to spare until noon, and went out for a city tour.

On finding an enormously tall building with its top flashing on and off like a lighthouse in the middle of the city, we thought it was the mighty Sears Tower; but it was a building of one hundred and two stories. Therefore, we took an urban bus to find the tallest building.

I asked a person sitting by me in the bus, "How can I get to the Sears Tower?" Every person, white and black, young and old alike, explained eagerly how I could get there. "Okay, that's enough. Thanks a lot," I said repeatedly. They were so kind-hearted to a foreign stranger.

I found the Sears Tower standing on the edge of Lake Michigan. When I took the elevator, it went up to the lookout on the 103rd story in a minute or so. Through the windows of the observation floor, I could see over the dazzling ripples of Lake Michigan, which looked like a sea rather than a lake, and I had a grand view of the city of Chicago down below. It was a really impressive and exciting moment. The sea-like lake water glittered with white spears of bright sunshine, moving in blue and white waves. Flowing through downtown Chicago, there was the small River of Chicago.

Around noon, Dr. P and his wife and I rode back to Detroit in the train.

To my mind, America looked like a free country-the country of free competition, free sex, and a free way of living.

On and off the university campus, the kindness of some American people, and their willingness to help others deeply moved me. They were kind, openhearted and bright, and honest and diligent as well.

Once, when I asked a young girl how to find a place I wanted to visit in downtown Detroit, the pretty girl said, "I'm sorry, I don't know." She then went to another passer-by and asked, then returned to me and told me the direction.

Every time people's eyes met with those of a foreign stranger, they said, "Hi," or "Hello," with a friendly smile. A Korean college teacher was supposed to have thought that when a pretty-looking American girl said "Hi" with a nice smile on the university campus, she must have felt some affection for him; but he did not understand the openhearted manner of American greeting.

They seemed to study and work hard with a light heart, and were always ready and willing to help other people.

Though I was really busy studying day and night, I tried to visit many places in the States-as many as I could. First, I visited a cider press and apple orchard, and then an atomic power plant along with some of the university staff and other foreign students. I thought, of course, that studying diligently seemed to be very important; but it seemed that seeing American things would also be significant for me during my stay in the USA.

The chairperson of the English Department told me I should study more hours than the American students should for my MA degree. Therefore, I decided to transfer to Florida after the fall semester.

Unlike the W university, most of American universities seemed to be located in the remote countryside or woods. A fair number of dwelling houses were also located among trees or woods, almost not visible at a casual glance from outside. That is why most Americans wanted to have weapons with them at home, living as they did in remote or lonely places in the woods, I guessed vaguely.

After the semester ended, I traveled with Dr. and Mrs. P, and another Korean, Mr. Cha, on a Greyhound bus pass from Detroit. We traveled for about fifteen hours by Greyhound bus, and finally got to Washington, DC. We visited the back garden of the White House first, and found that only the trees in the back garden of the White House were white with snow. There was no snow in any other places except the back garden, and I asked a police officer on duty the reason. "That's the artificial snow for Christmas, you know," said the officer.

Then we went to the Washington Monument. There were numberless pigeons flying about near the monument, cooing sadly. Inside the monument, there was a police officer on duty, and we all walked up all the stairs to the lookout, which was like a city square. "Everyone thinks it's too big to fit on the top of this monument," Dr. P said.

Through the windows on all sides, we looked out on every part of the capital city. After that, we went to the Abraham Lincoln Memorial located to the south of the city.

In the open space behind the White House, a black youth yelled out to the visitors. "Satisfaction guaranteed! Satisfaction guaranteed!" He was collecting tourists to ride in his car on a sightseeing trip. "It's only ten bucks for the whole sightseeing trip around the city, okay?" the young black continued to yell; but no one seemed to want to ride in his car. At that moment, there came a tramcar, and all the people got on the long tramcar, and began a sightseeing trip around Washington, DC.

I remember that it cost me only five dollars, and we could freely get on and off as we pleased, and could see various tourist attractions all day long, including the Watergate building, and Arlington National Cemetery.

As night fell, Washington looked almost the same as Detroit or Chicago, crowded with dark-skinned people, and we started out for New York.

After a seven-hour ride in a bus, we finally arrived at the gloomy New York Greyhound bus terminal, with its aggressive atmosphere. There sat a few of rough-looking black people and Mexicans, giving us all strange looks.

Then Mr. Cha, who was well dressed, with his hair plastered with pomade, walked slowly into the restroom with a little swagger. All the eyes at the terminal turned upon him.

After a while, I too entered the restroom for men, and sat on a toilet bowl, when suddenly, there was heard a harsh voice from the next cubicle, "Down! Down! Down! Hurry up!"

Well, I did not know what in the world happened in that dirty place, but I hurriedly got out of the restroom and away from all the mental unease.

In a minute or so, Mr. Cha came out looking deadly pale from the restroom. He looked bewildered and shocked to the last degree. He confessed a thief robbed him of one thousand dollars he had kept hidden in his underwear, after stripping off his clothes and threatened by a black and a Mexican with a knife and gun, poking him in the ribs.

Therefore, we all agreed to report to the police station on the second floor of the bus terminal. All of a sudden, many police officers ran busily back and forth and picked up a dozen young suspects.

The police had Mr. Cha seated inside a small room, and each suspect was made to stand outside before a narrow glass window in turn to be seen from inside in the room. Mr. Cha just said, "Probably," or "Possibly," unsure of whom he had seen in the restroom. They all looked alike to him so he could not find out the real criminals.

Finally, a police officer asked us, "What made you all come here to New York?"

"We are all Korean tourists from Detroit," we answered.

Then two police officers told us to ride in the police patrol car, and we went to the City Hall to have a talk with a prosecutor. Then, as we requested, they took us to the Empire State Building, the most famous building in the world. The red nameplate looked beautiful on the front surface above the gate. Yes, all the world's VIPs had praised the world-famous building for its grandeur and beauty with one voice. Of course, the Sears Tower is now higher than the Empire State Building, but the latter has been the very symbol of American wealth and pride for the world.

We sat in a cozy coffee shop near the building for a while, and a young server offered another black coffee free to all of us. Then, we got on the elevator to go up to the observation floor on the 102nd story. The elevator seemed to move up eternally; slowly, slowly, it went up, and stopped at the 80th story. Here we got off, and transferred to another elevator. I do not remember the exact story, but we found a sturdy police officer, watching carefully everyone's face, maybe two or three stories below the observation floor.

The lookout was a small piazza-like place with loopholes in the wall. The views of New York City were incredible-a uplifting picture of unbelievable buildings. I felt almost dizzy and faint, feeling a kind of thrill and unrest in my mind.

Truly, I had been keen to get to the top of the Empire State Building from my childhood, and my young dream had at last come true. However, my first impression of New York City was a dark and rather gloomy one, with my unexpected yet unforgettable memory of violent robbery at the public bus terminal. We hurriedly said goodbye to New York before dark, and started for Niagara Falls.

Through the night, we were traveling to Buffalo, thinking of the families we had left behind in the home country. When the day broke, we arrived at Buffalo. Interestingly, during the ride in the bus, a Canadian citizen and an

American person were sitting together in adjoining seats. They were arguing about their own respective falls being more beautiful than the other one, with loud voices. The older American person said, "The American falls are much more wonderful, sure enough," and the Canadian retorted, "No, the Canadian falls are much more beautiful, and everyone knows that but you."

It was Christmas Eve when we got to Niagara Falls from Buffalo via a connecting bus. Everything looked white, as it had snowed deeply through the night; it was a white Christmas Eve.

The Niagara Falls seemed to be a great miracle of nature. The roaring sound of the enormous waterfalls expressed the wonder of nature, one of the greatest the Creator had ever made on earth. Really, it was an unbelievable sight. The strength, the formidable roar of water like the sea, and the force of nature truly was a miracle.

The bowed American falls, and the horseshoe-shaped Canadian falls...these two great cascades were releasing enormous quantities of water down below, forming a mighty, wonderful river, which ran down fast in a swirling torrent.

Before this great wonder of nature, human beings looked like ants, miserable nothings, standing by the cliff near the falls; and that may be the view of Oriental people towards nature, which is an object of divinity.

Well, innumerable visitors were standing on the edge of the American falls, looking insignificant like ants or dots.

As the weather was so cold, and it snowed a lot, there were not many tourists, and the place almost looked deserted. On Christmas Eve, I stood on the cliff by the Niagara Falls, looking down over the greatest wonder of natural creation.

There were two observation towers, and there was a connecting bridge between the two countries, called the Rainbow Bridge, a romantic and beautiful red-colored bridge.

All the visitors could pass over the bridge without a visa from the US to Canada, except people from a few countries, including Korea. Dr. And Mrs. P could go over the beautiful Rainbow Bridge to Toronto in Canada, as they had visas in advance through an arranged interview with the ambassador stationed in the States.

Mr. Cha and I had to return to Detroit by Greyhound bus via Cleveland.

During my stay in the USA, I made great efforts to see many American things. Therefore, Mr. Cha, and I, though robbed of one thousand dollars and a golden wristwatch in New York, continued to cross the American continent by bus, riding mostly by Greyhound. The Greyhound buses went very fast and were comfortable, with a small restroom in the rear; they used to stop near a cafeteria for meals three times a day, and so long-distance travel presented no problems.

At night, I could lie asleep on the seat if it straightened out to its fullest. We two crossed the vast continent in that way, day and night, over several days. We went along by way of Toledo, Chicago, and many other cities, when suddenly an American youth seated by me said, "That's the Rocky Mountains," pointing to a range of mountains that stretched away as precipitously as walls. The soaring, wall-like Rocky Mountains rose so high that they almost obscured the bright daylight.

This grand sight made a great impression upon me. The belief was that the well-known Rocky Mountains formed the watershed of westward progression for the cowboys. In the past, they took a breath at the Rockies for a while, and then rushed on toward the Wild West.

The Greyhound kept on going westward almost endlessly. Then, suddenly, a long bridge appeared before our eyes, and it was the longest bridge in the world-the Bay Bridge, which had replaced the Golden Gate Bridge in world fame because of its length. It seemed to take almost thirty minutes crossing the bridge.

When a Korean student was telling his advisor his plan to travel across the continent, using the semester break, the professor said in a confident manner, "You'll see the world." This revealed the strong inclination of the cowboy people to have the best or the world's No. 1 country. The American cowboy has looked upon his world as the place of his 'Manifest Destiny'-his natural right to rule and lead the world in his own way. Emerson and Whitman proclaimed this in a positive voice. To them, the vast continent itself was poetry for reciting aloud.

In San Francisco, we visited the beautiful Golden Gate Bridge. In front of the bridge, many colorful flowers were in full bloom, even in winter; but the weather was warm, almost like springtime in Korea.

I had once watched a soap opera on TV in Korea, just before going to the States, in which a hero said somewhat boastingly that he had walked across the entire bridge. Well, the bridge looked beautiful, and deserved to be world-famous, I thought. The bridge went across straits in the Pacific Ocean, looking picturesque and misty, as the beautiful symbol of American wonder and technology.

Mr. Cha and I felt dead tired and very hungry. On our way back downtown, we met a kind-hearted Korean woman, who asked us to have a Korean meal at her house. Strangely, the houses here stood side by side with the same appearance and size. This kind woman treated us to delicious Korean foods such as rice, Kim chi, and plenty of other dishes.

After our many thanks to our new friend, we went to Fisherman's Wharf, and then rode on the famous streetcar, pulled along over the city slope by cables under the ground. Standing on the Fisherman's Wharf, I viewed the beautiful Golden Gate Bridge looking misty over the ocean, thinking the impressive sight was almost a picture-postcard heaven.

Nevertheless, the heart of downtown San Francisco seemed dark and violent, especially at night. As we walked along the central streets, we heard a strange obscene moan from a nearby movie house. Mr. Cha wanted to see the adult movie, but we had too little time to enjoy a sex movie there.

Later, we went down to Los Angeles by bus, and at around midnight, we arrived in the 'city of angels'. Apparently, Mr. Cha called some Korean acquaintances by phone, but failed to receive an invitation for a home cooked meal by any of them. It seemed that every Korean was too busy living his own life in the States, occupied deeply with his own life struggle. Truly, for a lonely Korean student, an invitation for a traditional Korean home-cooked meal was the greatest favor he could get from the Korean residents.

During our transcontinental travels, Mr. Cha was worried and felt terrified every time he had to go to a restroom, maybe recalling the terrible memory of his robbery in New York.

Usually, even in a crowded terminal, there was standing

a big police officer on guard with a gun and nightstick at his waist near any public restroom. Frequently he would go inside to see if there was any trouble, or if any sly person had hidden himself in there with a weapon. Even in an overcrowded bus terminal, vicious people would hide themselves in the restroom, and threaten to kill anyone coming in there to answer a call of nature. They used hideous weapons, and asked for money or other things of value.

In such a very dangerous environment, and with such disorderly public security in the big cities, no one, especially foreigners, dared to walk around downtown. An American citizen once said," If anyone walks out into the heart of big city alone, especially at night, he will soon be disappeared like wind before your eyes."

Every time Mr. Cha had to go to relieve himself, he would ask me to go there with him, and as soon as he had finished, he'd run out of the restroom like a frightened rabbit. Sadly, that was the real picture of American public security. This was a sad story, indeed. Was this the world's No. 1?

We were wondering why the black people stared fiercely at Asian people, even in public places, such as a bus terminal or train station. It was said they believed Oriental people had lots of cash on them; and in Detroit, a Korean student had told my roommate, "If you have one hundred dollars on you in cash, and walk downtown alone, your life would not be yours anymore, you know." Then he added, "I always carry twenty dollars with me, and every time a rough villain threatens to kill me, I'm ready to give the wretched man the banknote. It's a kind of safety measure for surviving in this country."

Mr. Cha and I visited the overcrowded Universal Studio, the center of American cowboy movies. It was teeming with tourists and their kids just like other well-known tourist attractions around the world.

After that, he said goodbye to me, and went to Las Vegas, but having a little time to spare, I went back to Detroit alone via Arizona, New Mexico and the desert areas, Springfield, and Chicago again. I was following Highway 66, as Tom Joad's family did in John Steinbeck's *The Grapes of Wrath*.

During my four days' bus trip across the continent, I felt lonely, as if I was standing alone in this vast world under the cloudy sky all by myself, threatened by impending dangers both from within and without. I was all alone on the vast continent.

Really, I had never felt as lonely and desolate as that before in my whole life. Sometimes, a gloomy thought flashed across my mind what if I met a wicked gangster in a strange place. Moreover, during my bus travels, I tried not to miss what the bus driver was saying while driving, in case I had to transfer to another bus. If I did not, I might get on a wrong bus and go to Texas instead of Detroit!

Four days after I had left LA, I got back to the snowbound city of Detroit. I felt tired and very lonesome in my mind, but there were several letters awaiting me from my wife, my family, and former teachers in Korea. They were full of love and warm-hearted goodwill for me.

After reading these kind letters, I felt encouraged again, and got ready to leave for Florida the next morning, to my next university.

CHAPTER 6
The Florida Sunset

On September 11, 2001, it was a fine autumnal day. I had no class, and after breakfast, I began to write my doctoral dissertation as usual.

Its main theme was about the relationship between man and nature, titled *The Central Meaning of Man and Nature in Poetry-With Special Reference to Nature Poets: William Wordsworth and Robert Frost.*

As the thesis was due around the end of December, I was stepping on it.

In three hours or so, I had a coffee break awhile, and turned on TV absent-mindedly.

There was a cut-in on a plane accident in New York City. I thought it could be a common case of plane crash at first; but shortly I found that it was far from being such kind of a plain accident.

There was a surprising news flash on the willful plane clash into the World Trade Center. Most surprisingly, a passenger plane plunged into the heart of northern WTC building; and in that very instant, a fiery flame was being raised like a cloud, and then the mighty 110 storied skyscraper fell to pieces on the ground incredibly enough. Moreover, in a short while, another passenger plane made an onrush at the southern WTC building, and it dropped to pieces with a crash all of a sudden.

The unbelievable total collapse of the World Trade Center twin buildings in a row within a few minutes... They were the very symbol of American economic power and strength, standing highest in New York City, the central city of American economy as well as the world trade and business.

The two soaring symbols of American economic power crashed into pieces instantaneously... They dropped to pieces by the crazed clash of passenger airplanes purposely by and by. The innocent passengers on the planes became the victims of Japanese, kamikaze-like surprising attacks in spite of themselves.

There was repeated news show of the unbelievable worst terrorism in a series. The unbelievable scenes of two consecutive plane clashes, followed by the abrupt fall of twin buildings ran on television repeatedly for several days.

Who in the world could dare to use civilian airplanes and innocent passengers as missiles and involuntary suicide bombers?

Besides the most wicked attacks on WTC twin buildings, the dammed terrorists also waged a surprising attack on the Pentagon by the third kidnapped plane clash against it, almost the same as on WTC buildings.

The powerful symbol of American military strength collapsed miserably. Reportedly, the fourth attempt for the worst terrorists to attack the White House failed in vain, owing to the thwarting act of bravery of some passengers on board for their dear lives against the inhuman beings. The White House has been the very symbol of American politics, making a central role in the worldly affairs.

Some say that the September 11 was the worst day of infamy throughout American history. It was the day when two unknown enemies hit the very heart of the sole world superpower: unseen and from the inside.

Even though Japan had once launched a surprise attack on the Pearl Harbor in 1941, it could be unlikely in the least that the American continent got rained hard blows on its chest coincidently. Truly, it was for the first time in its history that the American mainland was under attack. The three main symbols, the spirit buildings of American politics, military strength, and economic power were under the surprising attacks simultaneously.

In addition, who could imagine the fact that this world superpower might have got this kind of unthinkable offensive from unseen terrorists within the country?

While I watched repeatedly the TV coverage of terrible scenes for several days, I came to know that the vicious suspects had studied aviation in Florida, the sunshine state, where I finished my MA degree in English in my thirties.

I wondered why the ones trained in the beautiful Florida to commit such kind of the worst, unpardonable crimes to the guiltless American people in the world.

Where could they be called human beings like us? No! They were nothing but the dammed evil spirits born into this world with the fiendish brutality in their nature, I thought.

Even amid the terrible horror, many American people performed the various acts of bravery as many as they could for the wounded and the killed. Americans mourned their dead. They would quite naturally prepare to fight back, soon launching a lethal retaliatory strike against unknown foes inside and outside the country.

Stood America united!

Showing the flags of Stars and Stripes in the sea-like waves, they rose to the national crisis altogether. Americans attended candlelight vigil across the country, and realized they were at war.

On watching the saddest mourning in America, I recalled the things past during my stay in the sunny Florida state for my graduate work more than twenty years ago.

After returning from my transcontinental travel for several days, I left Detroit for Tallahassee in Florida by Greyhound the following morning. From the snowy North, the bus kept going down toward the Deep South for almost thirty-five hours.

When the bus stopped awhile at a bus terminal, all the blacks glared at me as they had done before in other cities. Dr. P had once said to me, "Look away. Do not meet their glares. Pay no attention to them, you know?"

Every time I felt someone stare in a shop or public place, I would find blacks glaring at me, standing outside in silence. In Richmond on a summer night, when I was entering the men's room at the bus terminal, two black youths imitated me falsely at the entrance, giggled for a minute and caught me by my hand, asking, "How're you doing?" as if they were testing me something. When I answered, "How're you doing?" they seemed to think awhile; then they slowly released my hand, and went off.

After about two days' travel, I finally arrived at a small, warm city located in northern Florida. This was Tallahassee, the capital city of Florida, the sunshine state.

The F University was located in the center of this small city, looking somewhat ancient but bright with buildings of red bricks. Under the bright sunshine, there were avenues of palm trees. Various flowers, such as azaleas, and winter camellias, were in full bloom around the university campus. As in California, the winter weather was like the springtime in South Korea. In the Northern States, it was snowing heavily, but it was as warm as spring in Florida.

As I had expected, I was to share an on-campus apartment room with a young Japanese student.

When I first met him in the room, this sly-looking young man asked me, "Where're you from?" When he heard I was a Korean, he made an ugly face, and I felt a dislike for him too, in spite of myself. A Korean can hardly have a liking for wily Japanese. The two peoples do not like each other-it is in their nature, I think.

I walked around the university campus, and happened to meet a queer-looking student with mustache from India. He kindly told me some information about the university and the city of Tallahassee. Then, I walked along about a mile to the shopping mall, and bought some utensils and foods including rice and vegetables. Instead of eating at the university cafeteria, I chose to cook for myself, using Korean food if it was available.

One morning, I asked the young Japanese out of sheer courtesy, "Please have a meal."

He replied, "No, thank you. That is no good."

He used to come back to the apartment every night in the small hours, and that was around the time when I went to bed. On and off, lying awake in bed before sleep, we exchanged a few meaningless words, and the rude Japanese youth always spoke ill of South Korea and Taiwan to me; but he praised North Korea highly, and Red China, the communist countries. He even said once,

"Koreans are dirty, and ill-natured."

Every time he spoke to me, he always sided with North Korea, blaming South Korea for everything.

Naturally, I felt very displeased in my mind, but tried not to be angry with him. He used to speak badly of South Korea and Koreans at all times, but respected America to a ridiculous degree, almost blindly. He was revealing the archetypal Japanese national mentality-'to be haughty before the weak, and humble before the strong.'

One night, I made up my mind to let this wicked boy know the truth about his country and people, on purpose.

As one of weak points of the Japanese people is in their poor articulation of English, I could hardly understand what he was talking about; and I abruptly advised him, "Hey, pack up your things, and go back to your country right now, and stop wasting your time and money any longer. It would be good for you on every account. You got it?"

"What are you talking about now, mister?" he cried out, surprised.

"As you might know well, the Chinese are much better than you Japanese in pronouncing English. When I studied in Detroit last year, most American students seemed to have a deep interest in the Chinese character. I thought then the Chinese professor had a fairly good pronunciation of the English language; but the students would complain in the class, saying that they had an interest in the Chinese character, but could not understand what the teacher was talking about in the class."

"But this Chinese professor has nothing to do with me, you know," said the sly Japanese in his rotten voice.

"Yes, he has, sure enough. The Chinese teacher spoke relatively good English, but provoked many complaints among the students. Now I can tell you you are speaking the worst English in the world. I do not think you will be able to receive a Ph.D. in your major at an American university in the future, and even if you do get a degree, you will never be a college teacher in the States, as you want, with your poorest English pronunciation. Even if you talk for about two hours, I can hardly catch a few words correctly. In my opinion, that is not English at all, only stuff and nonsense in both meaning and pronunciation as well. So, I advise you frankly to return to your home country now, and that's all."

Lying in my lonely bed, I then continued to attack the ill-mannered Japanese student for two or three hours.

At last, the ugly Japanese student when undone by me, said, "I'm defeated by your logic, mister."

Then I fell into a deep sleep. However, thinking it over, I was very unhappy after my unpleasant argument with this wicked youth, and guessed that he would never speak to me from then on.

I was full of loneliness, with no one to rely on, struggling desperately in this vast foreign country, at the opposite point from Korea on the globe, and worst still, my Japanese roommate, who was rude and cunning by nature, was not speaking to me, even though we lived in the same room.

Yet the next morning, quite contrary to my expectation, the wicked young Japanese said politely, "Good morning, mister. You do not use my car when you go shopping. I do not understand why not. Will you drop in at my office after school?"

He was expressing some heartfelt kindness to me for the first time since we had met. He had a cheap used car, and apparently worked as an assistant in a professor's office.

Dumbfounded at first by his unexpected change of attitude, I wondered what made him turn around like that. Then I said calmly, "No, thank you."

Mostly, they say, Japanese people are narrow-minded, egocentric, double-faced and cunning by nature; but they are also diligent, clean and kind, especially to the strong.

They say these people have an awe of strong figures engrained in their archetypal national unconscious. Douglas Macarthur was once worried about the Japanese people having a death-defying antagonism toward the American occupation forces stationed in Japan after the Pacific War; but quite contrary to his worry and anxiety, all the Japanese people, kneeling down in the dirt, welcomed the US soldiers wholeheartedly. Really, they are very odd people.

The Japanese women were busy selling their bodies for money to GIs, and some Japanese people regarded Macarthur as their 'god of war', to the ridicule of the world.

However, the essence of the archetypal Japanese pattern has been their cunning double-faced character, that is, their 'Judas kiss'. Before anyone strong or superior, especially foreigners, they show their heartfelt obedience, but betray them behind their backs.

Kneeling down on the ground, they showed their strange and oddly cunning nature as people who would betray the American occupation soldiers; but it was far from being their true sentiment, only their strange pattern of national feeling. Stealthily, they try their utmost to observe and learn all the merits the strong possess, as much as they can and then, look for every chance to betray and conquer the strong, if possible. It could be strategy of a cunning and treacherous people.

The unchangeable, archetypal Japanese mentality lies in the national slogan, 'Let every nation take its proper station'. This reveals their shrewd expansionism, which is similar to the American cowboy's 'Manifest Destiny' in its reality.

As would be expected, the sly-looking Japanese youth

was slowly growing ruder in his attitude, little by little; and one night I severely scolded him once again for his treacherous 'obedience'.

One sultry summer day, when I had returned from a weeklong trip around the Southern States, I found my room terribly hot. I asked the manager the reason, and she came to my room and told me not to touch the thermostat. I came to realize that the wretched Japanese boy had turned it to hot from cool in that sultry weather, and then had run off like a ghost, to be transferred to another university.

F University had the quarter system, instead of semesters as at W university in Detroit. Usually, in a school that uses quarters, school days were about seventy days, exams took ten days, and the rest was the quarter break. I took three graduate courses in literature, and unlike in Detroit, most of the open courses in Tallahassee were in literature.

When I attended the first class meeting of 'American naturalism', I could hardly understand what the professor was talking about, but to my delight, there was another foreign student from Greece, who outwardly looked almost like an American. He was majoring in creative writing for his MA. He seemed to have little difficulty in understanding in class, and helped me a lot in every difficulty.

Wondering what I had studied in my home country before coming to the US, I struggled desperately to catch up with my fellow classmates. I read and read, and tried to read novels as fast as I could all day long, except for sleeping hours. Mostly, one literature course had ten novels as the required texts, a thesis called a 'paper', along with mid and final exams, and a quiz or pop test as well.

As at W university in Detroit, I was the only Oriental student, and when I entered the English Department, located on the third floor of the Williams Building, all eyes focused upon me, and I was full of loneliness, listening with difficulty during class because I was a foreigner.

I had to read and read, studying in this foreign land almost with a death-defying spirit, as if I had been groping in the dark. Prof. C, one of my former teachers in South Korea, once told me, "You should study in the States with a death-defying spirit-to do or die."

In addition, my graduate studies at K University in Seoul were a help to me.

The old professor of American folklore always had his class late at night, bringing a big tape recorder with him into every class meeting. In the folklore class, they told us the story of blue-colored ghosts and the terrible massacre of Indian tribes by WASPs in the frontier days, and the professor often made all the students listen to his recorded ballads, poems, and stories, which sounded dismal and blue, going well with the night air.

Every morning, after a hurried meal, I used to attend

classes, and for the rest of hours, apart from sleeping time, I would squat down on the campus grass near the palm trees. I read the pile of novels as quickly as I could; I was absorbed in books totally, not caring about the passing of time at all.

When I stopped reading, I would often find lights on in every building and lamp on the campus, and darkness all around me. Then, I would get slowly up from the grass, and make my way back to Rogers Hall, my apartment block.

Well, there was an attractive young Korean girl student from Seoul. I met her at the first orientation meeting just after I had transferred from W university in Michigan. She seemed to like me at our first encounter, and I was so lonely that I felt like having a girlfriend in my heart. Nevertheless, I was determined to give up every other thing, concentrating on my graduate studies, overcoming every difficulty and solitude with a will.

Day in and day out, I just read and read novels, wrote papers, preparing for exams and tests, I struggled desperately at my studies. In a sense, I could barely feel lonely and homesick, faced with terrible burden of work I had to do.

Yet in the midst of such a hard life, I would often feel refreshed by the bright smiles of the young and pretty girls working part-time in the library whenever I tried to borrow books.

One day, the folklore professor told all the students to submit a research paper on indigenous folklore; and so, I dropped into the college of arts library in the hope of gathering some useful material on Korean folklore.

The girl who sat at the desk in the book circulation section, looked especially beautiful, and I felt very much cheered by her bright smile and kind words, "Thank you for borrowing many books like this," as she beamed at me.

In Florida, young girls used to sunbathe even in January, which went well with the name, 'sunshine state'. Around the campus, and near the university apartments, countless well-made, charming girls would lie down half-naked on the campus greens, enjoying their sunbathing in the balmy winter weather.

The casual sight of a young woman taking off her clothes right down to the smallest white panties and bra, and then stretching out on the grass in the campus embarrassed me. Then I would recall an American film I had seen in my college days in which the hero would repeatedly say, "This is a free country."

Well, America was a free country. No one seemed to care about other people; they just went dutifully about their own business. I think, this free American democracy is based upon individualism and capitalism...They have the natural right to look for their individual happiness, and enjoy life with light hearts.

I felt little mental stresses during my stay in the US apart the heavy burden of work I had to do, and most Americans were kind and ready to help other people willingly.

A Korean student staying in Chicago sent me a lengthy letter, saying he had been feasting his eyes in his spare time in the third floor of tall apartment building and enjoyed looking down upon the half-naked girls lying on the grass from his room.

Most of girls looked attractive, lively and bright with radiant smiles. All the Koreans I had met in the States would say with one voice that American girls deserved 'women first' in their country, without doubt.

I thought in mind that the people in the Northern States seemed more liberal than they were in the Southern States about sex. In the North, there were many adult movie houses scattered around every city, but down here, I could hardly find such a movie house, especially in the Deep South, including Florida. In a sense, the Southerners seemed more conservative, and the Northern people more openhearted and liberal. Sometimes, in Michigan, Koreans enjoyed sex movies, for a reasonable fee; and I too had a free ride from kind-hearted passing motorists when I was on my travels.

As the winter quarter was over, I decided to travel

across Florida with a Greyhound Florida pass using the short quarter break. However, during my trip around the sunny state, the thought of doing badly in my final exam in folklore distracted me; I was worried about getting a probable C in the test.

As I had done in my former travels across the continent, I went around the beautiful state of Florida, slept in the bus at night on the extended seat, and had meals at a cafeteria.

On a fine spring day, the smart Greyhound left Tallahassee for the far south. We kept going smoothly southward for hours, then we stopped unexpectedly along the route, and the bus driver said aloud, "The Suwannee River!"

Then, I was depressed by the thought of my failed exam in folklore, and failed to hear the correct words, only recalling dimly 'Swann's Way', the first volume of Marcel Proust's *Remembrance of Things Past*, which I had read for the modern European novel course of last quarter. However, the next moment, I came to remember the song, 'Suwannee River', which I had learned in my middle school days.

I felt excited to see the river with my own eyes in this unknown country and place. I got off the bus, and looked at the narrow river flowing calmly through some thick woods. The river was colored almost dark blue, looking picturesque in the real sense of the word.

I kept going down along the western coast of Florida,

crossing the long bridge that runs between St. Petersburg and Tampa.

Florida has numerous beaches and resorts along its beautiful coastline, including Miami and Disneyworld.

Miami City seemed to be one of the largest cities in Florida. At a bus stop near the Greyhound terminal, I was standing for long, waiting for a connecting bus to Miami Beach. Yet every bus failed to stop for me, and just passed by, ignoring me. I asked a passer-by why.

"Please flag your arm at an approaching bus if you want it to stop for you," he advised me kindly, with a smile.

I began to flag my arm up and down toward an approaching bus, and finally managed to get on one. The bus crossed a bridge connecting Miami City and Miami Beach. Everywhere I saw avenues of palm trees, and the bright sunshine beamed down from a cloudless sky.

At first, I guessed vaguely the beach grew overcrowded with people swimming or sunbathing on the Miami Beach shore, as it is a world-famous beach. Nevertheless, it looked very quiet, almost deserted. Only a few people were sitting on the white sands, talking with each other, or calmly watching the blue waves. A few people were swimming in the sea. In the far-off distance on the horizon, some dot-like ships sailed toward Cuba.

There was a pretty-looking Oriental girl sitting on the beach alone; she looked like a Japanese girl, and I asked her to take my picture. Willingly she took a picture for me, and then three ugly-looking Cuban youths started staring at me, making nasty faces. I felt awkward, and the pretty girl stood up after a minute, and began to walk away alone. I felt sorry for her, and angry with the unpleasant, ill-natured young ones.

There were luxurious hotels standing in a line along the beach, and red roses were in full bloom under the radiant sunbeams along the stream running in front of the hotels; while at the back of hotels spread the blue and green of the Atlantic Ocean. The beach and resort looked calm and beautiful. I strolled along the quiet beach, and found many stones with holes lying in the sand. I picked up a stone as a souvenir.

After a few hours, I jumped on a Greyhound bus, getting to Key West around dusk that evening. I did not know where Key West is in the world, but got on the bus absent-mindedly.

Leaving Miami behind, I sat alone on my seat, along with a few other passengers on the bus. I felt lonesome and homesick, desiring strongly to be home sooner than I expected.

After a while, surprisingly, I found the bus was running fast along on a narrow causeway built above the ocean. It grew nearly dark around me, and I barely had any idea of where the silent bus was rushing.

Through the coal-black night, the bus continued along a causeway just above the seawater, which churned wildly in the dark. Not knowing where I was going, I felt lonely and uneasy unbearably, as if left alone in this wide world. On and off, several small islands appeared in the sea and narrow bridges stood up above the water, connecting islands with each other in a line from Miami.

Dim lights were visible in all the houses on islands, but the silent bus kept running on. The passengers began to get off one by one on every island, and finally when I turned back, I found no one else in the bus except the bus driver and me. However, the bus seemed never to stop; it just went on. I felt chilly in the night air and desolate in my mind.

Around midnight, at last, the bus stopped on an island called Key West, the biggest one of the chain of islands. The old black driver said, turning back toward me, "You can find an old hotel some distance from here to north, and ride a bus leaving for Miami tomorrow morning."

There squatted a small, ancient-looking hotel, a moss-grown inn on the northern edge of island. A house cleaner led me to a room without a door, and cost me twenty dollars for a night's stay. I felt somewhat dreary and restless, being alone on an unknown island, as a complete stranger. I lay in bed sleepless through the night.

The next morning, I got up hurriedly and went straight

to the bus stop, and got on a bus. The driver was a kind old man, the same black driver I had met last night; and before we set off, he said plainly, "There is a summer house that belonged to Ernest Hemingway in this island, and there are lots of his mementos in there."

However, I was feeling desolate and tired, and I decided to go back to Miami; and the bus started at the right moment. Unlike the previous night, I felt safe, even cheerful and delighted under the bright sunny sky of a balmy spring morning. The black bus driver continued to tell me kindly about Hemingway and his novels.

"They say Hemingway would often stay at Key West. He wrote his The Old Man and the Sea in there, using his own first-hand experiences in Havana, and the story of a Cuban fisherman."

The blue-deep ocean spread out around me; sea gulls were flying over the waves and in the clear sky. The sight was very picturesque.

Hearing what the driver was earnestly saying, I also felt that Hemingway could safely write a great work as The Old Man and the Sea in such a wonderful climate surrounded by superb scenery.

After arriving in Miami around three, I started out for West Palm Beach again. In two hours, I stopped at the beautiful beach; it was exactly five in the afternoon. On getting off the bus, I ran to a shop nearby the bus stop.

I happened to see some beautiful postcards displayed for sale in that small store window. They looked like a postcard heaven; they were wonderful cards.

Just then, the storekeeper was closing the door, and so I tried eagerly to buy some of the beautiful cards. "Can I buy those cards in there?" I asked the keeper.

"No, you can't."

"Why can't I?" I said uncomprehendingly.

"My store opens from nine to five. And now it's five after five-five minutes past closing, you know?"

"Well, you do your business to make money, right? Moreover, you are just closing the door. Why don't you sell me cards now, instead of talking to me like that?" I said to him accusingly.

"No, I can't. Our policy is still five."

He did not sell me the cards to the end, and I could hardly understand him at that time, but later, I thought vaguely it could have been the honesty and strength of the cowboy that made his country as what it is now. An ordinary citizen who owned a small store kept his policy faithfully as it was. However, I was very sorry not to be able to get the beautiful cards.

I was sitting at the edge of a lake awhile nearby the Greyhound terminal; it was around the dusk of a spring evening, and the sun was ablaze with light in the sky. In addition, asked by me, a passer-by took a picture for me kindly. After thank-you to her, I rose from the seat, and then got on a Greyhound bus half-heartedly.

When the Greyhound bus was just about to start, I felt like murmuring "Adieu!" from the lips in spite of myself. I felt sorry strongly as if I had left a dear love behind me unknowingly. Thinking again, it was the first time for me to feel a sense of loss or sorry like that.

Looking out of the bus window absently, I found the scenery seen from the window picturesque incredibly. The sun was just verging on the horizon; and both the sky and the seawater were blazing red. A vacant boat was lying on the beach aslant under the setting sun. It was a postcard heaven in the real sense of the word. To my great regret, I did not get some of the beautiful cards, but instead, I did see the fantastic Florida sunset with my own eyes.

On my going upward to Jacksonville by bus, I felt something wanting all the way. I felt sorry and missing in my mind, desiring to get back to Palm Beach. I wondered if I might have lived in that beach in my previous life, but God may only know, I thought.

At that moment, a thought occurred to me that an old, well-known Korean poet had once visited a temple, located in a deep mountain; on leaving the temple behind the next morning, he said later, he'd felt sorry and missing strongly as if he'd left his hometown, with even tears gathering to his eyes. He said that he might have lived in there as a would-be Buddhist monk in his former life, an Oriental view of knot and karma of Buddhism or Hinduism, which has turned out to be true in psychic science or parapsychology these days.

Like other big cities in the US, Jacksonville, the largest city in Florida, looked also black and barren at night. No one, especially Oriental people, could dare to walk around downtown at night; I just went through by bus.

I arrived at Tallahassee in the small hours of the night from Jacksonville; and I ran as fast as I could to my university apartment block, feeling afraid of a surprise meeting with rough men on my way from the bus terminal. Yet Tallahassee looked safer, compared with other big cities.

By the way, around evening on November 7, 2000, there appeared a news flash on TV in Korea, concerning the presidential election held in the US.

According to a Korean correspondent stationed in Washington, D.C., the Republican candidate, Mr. George W. Bush won the presidential election. Therefore, I simply thought that the long presidential election campaign resulted in the return of Mr. Bush to the White House in the end.

However, on returning home at night from a visit, I heard they had annulled his election. From then on, both camps of Republicans and Democrats continued to make a frantic struggle to win the presidency for more than a month. It was unprecedented. Mr. Bush won the election finally, thanks to the total majority of the Electoral College in the sunny state of Florida.

As the US had a deep connection to Korea so far, in almost every field such as politics, economy, national security, culture and so every Korean had a keen interest in the result of the presidential election in the States.

During that breath-taking, somewhat muddy competition between two political parties in Florida, I vividly recalled things past in that sunshine state. I missed Palm Beach, and desired to see again the Florida sunset, blazing red in the sky and on the seawater like a picture postcard heaven.

Reportedly, the ex-president, Mr. Bill Clinton, once said in his Alma Mater in November, 2001 that this on-going shock and awe of terrorism Americans have been suffering now might have been initiated because of their 'original sins' in the past. This included the numberless massacre of Native American Indian tribes, and the cruel slavery of black African people, along with the terrible evil-doings the Christian people had inflicted upon Islamic people and Jews in the several military Crusades of the medieval ages.

Some say with assurance, that Japan and the US are two countries with the heaviest bad karmas on earth, piled-up high like a mountain. The American white people killed mercilessly about fifty million native American Indians, the very host of the continent, as if they had been wild buffaloes, so that they may have built their 'second Adam's new paradise' on the vast American continent. Well, the whites were all the strangers from other countries, largely from England; but they murdered countless native Indian people, and robbed them of the American continent. Then also, they ill-treated the black people, conducting all kinds of evils and bad doings to them. For those reasons, the American cowboy seems to have had a strong sense of guilty feeling in the depth of his heart.

Moreover, most of American writers have dealt with this deep-seated sense of guilty conscience as the main motif for their writing, trying to depict the unbecoming love or friendship between the white and   the black people at all times...

As has been well known, Edgar Cayce, the American sleeping prophet in the 1920s, had predicted in his sleep about the forthcoming fall and decline of the USA. In addition, G.M.Scallion, a computer scientist living now in the States, has predicted about the forth-coming future of his country repeatedly. He reportedly said that the explosion of Mt. Rainier in Washington State would be the start of the fall of America.

Mr. A, I remember, once said to his members of his 'society of true man', "the 'a priori world' of Buddhism is already gone, and now is in the 'a posteriori world', the one of coexistence, instead of that of former conflict with each other. I believe the past a priori world was the era during which the western thought and idea prevailed, while this a posteriori world is to be governed by the Oriental thought of coexistence."

As had been said by Buddha, the world rules by the strict law of retribution, and in that sense, there seems to be little choice for the Japanese people. They have lived along so far as wicked and ill-natured as always, having neither guilty feeling nor regret at all for their past vices and evils toward the neighboring Asian countries and the USA as well.

The cowboy people, however, have tried for long to do good things to the peoples in need on earth. They acted as a would-be 'world police' to preserve freedom against communists for several decades.

In his lifetime, Mr. A used to say, "Well, the most important thing you should bear in mind is the fact that the future to come may be changeable; and so the future could be flexible to a certain degree. For that reason, we should first feel regret sincerely for our past faults, and repent of our sins sincerely. And then, if we live good-naturedly, helping others and in good harmony with people and nature also, with a positive view of the future in our hearts, the accumulated knotty karmas are to be lessened little by little and the predicted evils may be alleviated..."

According to modern parapsychology, a person of piled bad karmas is to live along a thorny life, thus going through a great deal of human sufferings, and so his negative karmas lessen to that extent only slowly. If he tries his utmost to do good things to other people in need at the same time, his piled-up karmas are to clear off more shortly.

Most of prophets in the East and West alike, would often say that their predictions would be flexible in time to occur; they may happen earlier or later than the predicted time; but the important thing to note is that they may be surely happening.

CHAPTER 7
Man, Nature, and Heaven

Tallahassee, the capital city of Florida, is a small quiet city of about one hundred thousand inhabitants in all, and appears covered with thick woods. Looking over the city from a lookout on a building twenty-two stories high, I found the city fully planted with trees and woods, except the shopping mall, university, and the streets stretching endlessly away.

I was so busy with graduate work to do that I could hardly feel lonely and homesick in mind.

Every evening, exactly at five, from the Burger King standing on the street just in front of Rogers Hall, I'd hear the somewhat romantic song by Beatles, 'Hey, Jude'. Its sweet repeated refrain was flowing into the balmy night sky; it always made me feel strangely and painfully homesick. Usually, I would look over at the burger house silently from my apartment room. All the young American men and girls were gathering in groups at the Burger King with the lights all shining brightly. The song flowed out into the open air, and all the bright girls and boys were fully enjoying their youth.

The night air felt cool and balmy; the burger house was shining brightly with the lights on.

Even now, after a lapse of more than twenty years from that time, the song 'Hey, Jude' is still ringing in my ears. In the days to come, I would like to go there again, recalling the memory of the faint sweet sound of that Beatles song from my bygone days. Now, I remember the long avenues of palm trees standing along the streets and the bright sunbeams pouring down over our heads in Florida...

Every day, after class, I always sat down under the shady cocoa trees on the campus green, struggling hard to read novels with a reading speed of at least 'thirty pages an hour' to catch up with the American students.

I was tired out in both mind and body, but I had to go ahead with a will, day in and day out. I was terribly tormented by James Joyce's *Ulysses* and Marcel Proust's biographical novel, *Remembrance of Things Past*. However, the American naturalistic novels were interesting and easy to read, compared with the European ones.

My wife in South Korea regularly sent me Korean ginseng flour. Every morning, I used to mix a spoonful of ginseng flour with hot water, making ginseng tea in the kettle. I would drink the ginseng tea several times a day, which made me feel light-hearted and refreshed.

One day, a black woman clerk at the university post office asked me, "What's it in your registered parcel?"

"Its Korean ginseng flour," I replied, and then added, "It's very good for one's health and sexual vitality, you know."

"Is it really? You mean it's good for renewing sexual energy?" she asked, showing a great interest in the Korean ginseng. She then said, "Is it also good for women? How much is it? I bet it's really expensive in price..." She said she would like to buy some ginseng for her husband and even for herself, but seemed a bit doubtful, giving a little shrug.

Really, my life was a kind of war with speed, my reading speed. Piled books were always waiting for me, and I immersed myself in my reading, not even knowing the flow of time around me.

One sunny afternoon, I happened to be sitting in a chair in the union lobby, and turning toward the university swimming pool to the south, I was surprised to find exactly the scenery and trees that I had dreamed about in Korea before coming to the US. I remembered the dream vividly, in which the view of sky and woods had appeared exactly same as that before my eyes. So was being here in Florida something predestined in my life?

It was a strange and mysterious coincidence. By the swimming pool, there were many young girls lying down upon the grass virtually half-naked. At that time, I felt America was 'a place in the sun' to live in, a free country with a bright outlook for the future.

In the spring term, I took three courses, including the

British novel with Dr. S, and transformational syntax.

After class, I used to ask a friendly American Ph.D. candidate to see if there was any test or assignment, I had missed in the class. I had a difficulty in listening; and a kind, black girl once suggested that I study with her, knowing I could not understand fully the lecture in class. Nevertheless, I read and studied very hard and got seventy-eight points in transformational syntax, taking third place among thirty American students majoring in English. The kind American student who sat by me was surprised to find that I had got better mark than he, who got seventy-three, and looked at me repeatedly in wonder.

On a spring afternoon, I happened to pass a professor's office at the school of library science, which was in the basement just under the main F university library. There, I found some American students swarming around the professor's office door, pointing to a picture that was stuck to it. Therefore, absent-mindedly, I wondered about this and looked at the picture. The moment I saw it, I felt deeply humiliated in spite of myself. The picture was showing two poverty-stricken old Korean peasant women, squatting down in the dirt just in front of a shabby-looking thatched house. Their dark, wrinkled faces, the awkward smiles of their toothless mouths, and the poor house gave me an unbearable repulsive feeling. A sarcastic title tag,

'Two Korean librarians,' was at the bottom of picture.

I decided to meet this unknown professor, and remained standing outside the office waiting for him. In about an hour, a small, pot-bellied middle-aged man appeared before me. He opened his office with a key, and entered his room. Then I stepped forward, and introducing myself, and stating my major and nationality, I asked him why he had put such an unfortunate picture on the office door, which had caused many sneering giggles among innocent students, giving them a somber and negative impression of Korea in the depths of their hearts.

Then I added that if he liked, I was quite willing to give him a more favorable picture of Korea. Murmuring something inaudible, he slowly removed the sad-looking picture from the door.

After that, I forgot about it completely.

In the summer term, I had to take bibliography at the school of library science as a compulsory course for graduation. The bibliography was a one-hour course, but Dr. B, the woman graduate director, told me to take a four-hour course at the school of library science, as the course was not open in the English Department during the summer session.

However, at the first class meeting at night that I attended for the required course, I was surprised at the strange irony of my encounter with the professor. The professor taking the course was the very person who had put the poor picture on his office door two months before.

To my surprise, he seemed to remember me, my family name, major and nationality, and other things. At first, he showed a cold shoulder toward me. What was worse, I could not understand at all about the use of computers in library science. Well, what is a 'pathfinder'? I hardly knew about computers at all, as computers were not in common use in Korea at that time. It seemed as if a primary school child was attending a science course in college. It looked as if I would be surely failed on that course, and worse still, the professor seemed to have it in for me.

I was in a very difficult situation.

Late at night, after the first class meeting, a heavy downpour began with strong gusts of wind. Having no umbrella with me, I had to walk along in the rain to my apartment. The weather was like my own heart-dark, clouded, and desolate to the last degree.

Strolling around in the room, I thought and thought, but had no idea of a way out of this morass. I lay down sleepless all night, and early in the morning, I got up, and went up to the office of the graduate director, Dr. B.

Entering her room, I cried out in despair why I had to be in this dilemma, being a foreigner. The director had asked me to take four hours at another college for just one hour in my major. In addition, the professor in charge of the required course was prepared to show cold hatred toward me, and I could not understand the course a bit.

I told her about the unfortunate picture, and added that the professor was the very person I had asked to remove the picture from the office door. As I was saying this, in complete despair, tears began to roll down my cheeks. The female director showed a surprising response to me, giving no answer at all. She merely continued to say, "You must take bibliography before graduation, and we have no class schedule for the course in this term."

Luckily, just then, Dr. S, the head of the English Department, came into the room." What's up, Dr. B?" he asked earnestly.

He heard the woman director's account of my problem, and said," Why don't you let Mr. Hahn take the S/U course in our department?"

The help of the chairperson easily settled the problem. The woman director said to me, "Please go to Dr. M, and take a one-hour S/U course for bibliography, okay?"

Around the end of the summer session, I got an S (satisfactory) for the troublesome bibliography from Dr. M and was thus able to receive my degree in English. Really, it was the most knotty problem I had to solve during my study in America. I had to finish my degree in the summer session as I had received some offers of a job as a full-time instructor from the several universities in South Korea.

In the summer, I took a computational linguistics course using the SNOBOL 4 programming language, even though I was a complete stranger to computers. I had to struggle hard to understand the professor in the class, and the old professor said to me kindly, "Don't worry, Mr. Hahn. I myself once went to Portugal for graduate study when I was young. I know your difficulty well. Please cheer up, and I'll help you with your work." Very kindly, he explained to me how to use the computer, and encouraged me to have more enthusiasm.

I decided to write my degree thesis, which was on the chronic problem inherent in English education in South Korea, using the SNOBOL 4 programming language, with a view to improving the knotty problem of teaching English in Korea. Hurriedly, I began to write up my thesis from the spring term, and I found that the computational linguistics and my earlier graduate studies in Korea were a great help to me.

Unexpectedly, I was praised for my hurriedly written thesis by my advisor, who said repeatedly, "Amazing, Mr. Hahn."

On a hot summer afternoon, I successfully made an oral defense of my thesis, and finally, I could get an MA in English at F University. My advisor, an elderly woman professor, said, "Congratulations! You did a good job."

It was then that my wife sent me lots of Korean dolls and

souvenirs; and I gave them to the professors and staff as souvenirs.

Well, at last the day had come when I could fly back to my family in Korea, having got through all the difficulties in a foreign country.

As I had some days to spare before going home, I left for Texas by bus, freed of all anxiety and mental care.

Starting out from Tallahassee, I went across to New Orleans, the city of Tennessee Williams' A Streetcar Named Desire, and arrived at Dallas, the place of the 'unforgettable moment' of Kennedy's tragic death. I saw the place with my own eyes.

After that, I jumped on a bus leaving for New York and it seems I fell asleep in spite of myself. After a few hours or so, I woke up to noisy giggles from some women on the bus. Turning round, I found an innocent-looking black woman and her five kids seated behind me. All the white women continued to laugh at them, clapping their hands wildly. The young black woman looked somewhat ashamed and awkward at all the noisy laughter, but wore a faint smile on her lips; her five kids sat nervously beside their mother.

An attractive white woman asked the black mother with an ironic smile on her face, "How many kids have you got?"

"Twelve," replied the black woman indifferently.

There arose a roar of laughter among white women. They found her innocent response very humorous. The nervous little kids just looked anxiously at each woman's face in turn.

Then the naive black woman added, "This is our first trip to New York." Really, the mother and kids looked full of great expectations about the unknown greatest city in the States. Just then, the terrible memory of the theft of Mr. Cha's possessions flashed across my mind.

The next moment, another white woman asked the black mother, "How many kids are you going to have, then?"

"Maybe twenty," the black woman said, shamefaced.

All the white women burst out laughing once again.

"Why do you have so many children?" the white woman asked again.

"I don't know. Maybe God knows."

The bus went on, passing through the endless fields of wheat, and got to Little Rock. One man said, "This is the hometown of General Macarthur," in a somewhat proud voice.

I slept overnight in the moving bus, and the next morning, I woke to find the bus crossing a bridge over a river.

"What's the name of this river?" I asked a man sitting by me.

"This is the River Mississippi, you know," he replied.

I heaved a deep sigh of relief in spite of myself. It had

been my sincere wish to see the Mississippi with my own eyes before going back to my home country, as this river must surely be the very home of American hearts and minds, and the wellspring of American literature and their tender love of eternity from the past, seated deeply in every cowboy's heart. The bridge almost looked like the old bridge in my hometown in Korea. It seems that every American cowboy feels homesick when he sees the River Mississippi.

The bus crossed the river, and there stood a large billboard poster, in which Elvis Presley was playing a guitar. It was the city of Memphis, the hometown of Elvis Presley.

However, like other big cities in the US, like Detroit, for example, Memphis looked desolate and barren, with lots of tall buildings in ruins and burnt down.

I returned to Tallahassee in about a week, and then went up to Georgia, the Carter country, again; but I found Atlanta too dangerous at night, and I just went directly back to my apartment.

Only a few days remained before I returned to my home country, and I bought some presents for my family and people close to me.

One day, a foreign-born student from the Middle East told me, as I was sitting in the students' lounge, "Hey, Mr. Hahn, that's Korea-your country, you know."

A soap opera was then on the air. It was 'MASH', about Korea during the days of the Korean War. The introductory scene appeared, showing a hilly and barren landscape. I had once viewed this shameful drama before, but I could not understand why it was so popular among the cowboy people. This sort of drama would only make a negative impression of Korea upon American hearts.

At last, one summer day I got on a Northwest Orient plane flying to LA via Atlanta. Through the window, I could look down on the city of Tallahassee with its lines of coconut palms, and the F university buildings receding slowly into the distance. Adieu! I said to myself.

After sitting overnight for several hours at LA Airport, early in the morning, I flew to Seattle again. After another wait, the Northwest Orient jet took off high in the air. When I looked down below the plane, I saw the beautiful city of Seattle was beginning to fade slowly into the distance. Just then, I suddenly felt sorry in my mind and said to myself, when will I ever be back here again?

After a long flight of more than ten hours over the sea-like clouds, I finally landed at Seoul Airport, and met my family safe and sound.

It was my first spell of graduate study in the USA, but I had a thought I might go back to the States for a Ph.D. in the near future.

After I came back from the US, I taught English at K

college in my hometown as a full-time instructor, hoping to go back again to America for a Ph.D. earlier than I had expected.

From early in the 1980s, I have felt a strong interest in the life in nature, that is, the natural life, and natural treatment, as I was also in poor health.

One night late in 1980s, a Korean medical doctor appeared on TV in Korea. He was somewhat thin in appearance, but looked honest and sincere in nature.

He was a middle-aged doctor, living in the hilly country in California. He had also studied the medical science in Korea, and then in Michigan and California.

On TV, he explained about chronic adult diseases with ease and confidence, putting a heavy stress upon a healthy mode of living in everyday life.

His well-known motto was, "There is no disease which is unable to be cured, only an unhealthy daily life."

He has been widely known among Korean people before now, engendering the so-called 'Dr. R syndrome'. Everyone knows his name and his theory of medicine, and remembers his famous medical words such as 'endorphin', and 'T-lymphocyte'.

Well, according to him, he had been an ordinary doctor making lots of money in California, a successful doctor in the conventional sense, but had always felt a kind of mental worry and anxiety in his deep unconscious: what if a cancer had grown within his body even as a medical doctor?

He once said on TV that one day, late in the evening, he had heard a strange and mysterious voice from somewhere in the sky while seated in his office. Now, I can hardly remember the exact words he heard, but everyone including me believed that he received a revelation from heaven.

From that time on, he gave up his successful career as a doctor, and started his life afresh, helping countless unhappy and chronic patients, who were almost unable to find cures from modern medical treatment, through his unique theory of natural life and treatment.

He said even his family had not understood his sudden switch to a hard life living in the hilly countryside, far from his rich career as a doctor in the city. Well, you can say that he chose heavenly love rather than money.

He promoted his 'NEW START' movement for the healthy life: N (nutrition), E (exercise), W (water), S (sunshine), T (temperance), A (air), R (rest), T (trust, or love).

Dr. R has always put an emphasis on a healthy life according to the natural providence, that is, the life of naturalness, with true love for others in mind. He says that of the eight letters the last 'T', which is trust in God and love for other people, is most important for everyone's health and happiness in this world. He maintains that the only thing welcomed and desired is love for others, in unlimited measure for us, with no need for temperance at all. If we love others, it makes our bodies healthy and strong. As Gandhi said, "No one can hurt you but yourself." It will only hurt our health if we hate other people.

Recently, Dr. R appeared again on TV, saying that these days in the United States, ultra-modern medical science was beginning to approach every kind of disease from the fundamental view of molecular biology. The greatest emphasis was upon the role of genes in any cell within the human body.

Each gene in a cell is composed of DNA, the chemical material, nucleic acid, unmovable by itself within the body. Yet American scientists have begun to call the mysterious, unknown force in the vast universe 'cosmic consciousness' which can make genes in our bodies move and function according to the providence of nature, or heaven's will, to keep our bodies healthy and strong.

Dr. R showed two shocking pictures to the Korean audience from the journal The American Scientist, published recently in the United States. One was a strange picture of a giraffe eating a dead animal's bone in the desert, and the other a picture called sex changing in mid-ocean. There is proof that the unbelievable phenomenon of changing sex occurs among fish in the ocean when there were only ten female fish left, turning half of them into male fish. As a gene consists of DNA, a chemical material, Dr. R asserts it can hardly move or function for itself. Yet strangely enough, half of the ten female fish turned into male ones, and the grass-eating animal of giraffe was unwittingly eating a dead animal's bone. Dr. R explains that the mysterious force in the vast universe could be the force of life or love, which makes genes move according to the nature's providence, as the gene responses to necessity and energy. This heavenly energy is the force of life or love of the Maker widely spread throughout this universe, just like bright sunbeams. Moreover, American scientists have called this force 'cosmic consciousness'.

Frankly, Dr. R as a medical doctor himself, has spoke frankly about the existing limitation of contemporary Western medical science, especially regarding chronic adult diseases, such as high blood pressure, diabetes, cancer, and even AIDS. He says even AIDS can be cured if one lives a healthy life according to the law of nature or Heaven, that is, cosmic consciousness-meaning the force of life and love between living beings, instead of hatred and destruction. He argues we should live a life of love and trust between ourselves; then the T-lymphocyte cells are strengthened surely enough, getting rid of diseases naturally. We should abandon any unhealthy life that is contrary to Heaven's law and God's love. We human beings have lived a life of hatred and struggle between ourselves-that is, a life of selfish egotism and destructive energy, as said by Freud.

His theory of medicine may be said to be the theory of 'healthy life', through which our T-lymphocyte and NKC(natural killer cells) can be strong enough to beat off any disease germs, making our physical bodies revert to their original basic structure; this will cure diseases fundamentally and naturally, instead of mere physical treatment of the visible symptoms. If we live with love for others, following the law of nature or Heaven, endorphins produce plentifully from within our bodies, making our T-lymphocyte cells stronger and stronger, and our natural killer cells (NKC) increase to a marked degree. Naturally, this may fit in with God's teaching to us, or the 'Spiritus Mundi', in W.B.Yeats's "The Second Coming", meaning 'spirit of the universe' or 'cosmic consciousness'.

He maintains the present limitation of contemporary medicine comes from the fact that doctors have tended to treat the symptoms of illness in hospital, not trying to turn the fundamental structure of the physical body and way of life into a healthier one. A healthy life could mean a more natural way of living in harmony with the natural providence or God's love (as witnessed in the Bible).

Without a beneficial change in our life from the present one against Heaven's will (God's will) and the law of nature, to a harmonious and kind-hearted way of living to go with the favor (love) of Heaven (God), we can hardly be healthy and happy before and after this gloomy turn of 20th century.

I was able to buy the whole videotape set of his lectures on the 'NEW START' about various chronic diseases last year; and through his tapes, I have continued to practice his theory of natural treatment for a healthy life.

He emphasizes we should live with 'Loveton', the force of love, instead of 'Saton', the force of Satan, and that is the way that Heaven (God) or nature tells us to live in this weary world.

A few weeks ago, I happened to see on TV that organic food is becoming very popular among Americans these days, and this almost matches Dr. R's theory of natural food and life as the basic idea.

This might be when every human being feels ill at ease about almost everything. This is especially true about the future of humankind and the earth. Many predictors, in both East and West alike, have warned us about the forthcoming catastrophe around the turn of century.

Now, I am teaching American and British poetry to college students as my majoring course. Of the many of romantic poets, William Wordsworth holds a view, which is naturally pantheistic, and says we can meet God in the lap of nature by praising and extolling nature in our lives.

He reveals to us the warm-hearted harmony of human being and nature as the ordinary, friendly ties between the two.

Students seem to like his well-known poem, *Rainbow* best of all of his works, and Wordsworth's natural view of life and God as well. To Wordsworth, nature is a warm, close friend and God too, as well as his eternal resting place in this troubled world.

In the middle of 1980s, I began deeply immersed in the natural philosophy in China, or Taoism of Lao-tze, which is in short the idea of flowing water as the flowing water could be the only substantial entity, which fulfills faithfully the law of nature. Its main idea is in 'doing nothing artificial, and following the rule of nature' just as water does.

For thousands of years, this Taoism has been deeply rooted in the depth of the ordinary Chinese people representing the true mentality of the Chinese. In my class, most students favored this natural philosophy, unlike Confucianism with its typical artificiality.

From the ancient times on, there has been numerous numbers of tactical books in both west and east as well. However, of them all, the Chinese people have read seven kinds of tactical books of their own, of which the *Sunz Tactical Book* has been the best, a magnum opus.

If we read the well-known ancient Chinese historical

novel, *San Ku Zu*, the war tales of three ancient Chinese kingdoms around 3rd century, we will soon be buried into the eventful, stormy stories of generals and strategists, which give an absorbing interest to us even now. Of them all, the strategist Kong-ming seems to be most heroic, and outstanding, who was the faithful follower of Sunz tactics.

Sunz once wrote the world-famous *Sunz Tactical Book*, and may have lived in China, in the fifth century B.C. His excellent tactical book, based upon the Chinese natural philosophy, first described the thought of Ta, Kong-wang, who had lived in the Chou Dynasty of ancient China in 11th century B.C. His thought inherited down to Lao-tzu, a contemporary of Sunz; and Sunz once systematized the natural philosophy of Ta, Kong-wang and Lao-tze into the unique strategic form, formulating his famous tactics.

Lao-tze said that the ultimate way of universe is Tao (way), unseen and unheard or untouched. Yet, the blessed Tao is achievable through humbleness, and identification with eternal nature. He also said that Tao conforms to the rule of nature, having in mind the spontaneous perfection of eternal nature. Closely related to Tao is Te, the force that imbues man with the natural qualities that he has, and which makes it possible for him to achieve Tao.

Lao-tze wrote two short books, called *Tao-Te-Ching*, the Book of Tao and Te, consisted of five thousand Chinese characters. It has some eighty-one chapters of poetic and mystical remarks on morality, virtues, way of life, and precepts of Taoism.

An essential element of his philosophy is his somewhat paradoxical notion of 'wu wei', doing nothing artificial and achieving much. The natural philosophy of Lao-tze lies in the idea of flowing water, which accomplishes Te (virtue) most faithfully in the universe of Tao, adapting itself freely to the natural law and circumstance.

When I was in thirties, I happened to meet an old Buddhist monk at a temple in the hilly countryside near my dwelling city. In addition, I said to the aged Buddhist monk that I would have felt a deep interest in the thoughts of Buddha, and Lao-tze. Moreover, when we parted after talks, he gave me two worn copies of Oriental strategy: those of Ta, Kong-wang, and Sunz. Then on and off, I read the ancient tactical books repeatedly; and then on I'd studied about the seven kinds of Chinese tactical books for almost twenty years.

Sunz set up the natural idea of water into his famous strategy, with a view to defending his country, thus having produced his outstanding *Sunz Tactical Book*. He thought that the stream of mind could be the same as the flowing water; he could catch and control the minds and hearts of his soldiers and even his enemy as he could do the flowing water freely, according to the philosophy of

Lao-tze. The flowing water runs freely following to the rule and order of nature, instead of certain kind of logic or reason.

This Sunz tactics has influenced all kinds of tactical theories and books in both east and west as well. His main tactical thoughts are economical, scientific, psychological, and political; and he gave a great influence upon Clausewitz, the Prussian expert on military science and strategy in 18th century.

Rommel, the famous German general of the African Corps, who had been called 'a fox in the desert' by the allied forces as the formidable being in the African desert during the World War II, was the admiring reader of Sunz tactics; and he once declared, "Victory is the culmination of deception."

Napoleon could barely be a born genius of military strategy and operation, and he too was a fervent admirer of the Sunz tactics; and most of his excellent tactics came from the Sunz strategy. By becoming a spiritual disciple of Sunz, Napoleon could be well versed in tactics, and thus, thought to be more than a human being in the art of war.

This Sunz tactics consisted of 13 chapters and regarded as the outstanding textbook of strategy not only in East but also in West. The German King, Wilhelm the Second once deplored after he had been defeated in World War I, "If I'd read this Sunz tactics only twenty years earlier..."

The late Chinese Communist Chairman Mao Tse-tung fought with Generalissimo Chiang, Kai-shek, having driven him into the narrow Formosa with his tactics similar to those of Sunz. Even though Mao was in the extremely negative situation, with the poorly trained, and equipped followers, most of who were farmers. Generalissimo Chiang was well educated in the US, and far from being an incompetent general. Along with the chronic corruption in the central government, Mao's quasi Sunz tactics sadly defeated Chiang.

In Vietnam, the poorly armed Vietcong fought against the American troops, trained, and armed with ultra-modern science and weapons, with the oldest Oriental strategy of Sunz.

Reportedly, according to a French magazine in 1987, the American Marine Corps Commandant General Gray had the Sunz tactics into the US officers' tactical textbook at the thought of sad withdrawal of American soldiers from Vietnam. It was the first defeat of American cowboy, which has tormented the proud cowboy people, having been the so-called 'Vietnam syndrome', the crisis of confidence.

Rousseau proposed his idea of 'return to the nature' for the happiness of human beings, away from the ill-natured, wicked life style of modern civilization, especially in big cities.

Like William Wordsworth, they called Robert Frost a

'nature poet'. The two poets are different from each other in their respective view of nature.

Frost praises nature in his well-known poem, "Stopping by Woods on a Snowy Evening"; but it reveals the modernity of his character with its rather negative viewpoint.

I think Frost's view of nature would be the one most of Western people have had in the past. To them, nature would be almost meaningless, unknowable, and even hostile, and as such, merely an object to be used and conquered. The people in the West have savagely destroyed nature under the pretext of development, resulting in the present serious environmental problems, including widespread pollution by land and sea.

The culture of materialism and mammon's in the West has now prevailed even among the people in the East, influenced by the West.

Many seers have warned of the forthcoming terrible contamination of air and the environment around the end of the century, including Nostradamus and the famous prophets in the East.

One day in the early 1990s, Mr. A asked me to join his society of 'True-man', consisted of fifteen members from various social strata.

Almost every time I went up to see him, I would meet one or two strange faces in his office. He had quite a few disciples, who tried to follow him and learn his special skills through spiritual vision.

Late in his fifties, Mr. A wrote many spiritual poems; and they asked me to translate his poems into English.

Here is a poem of his "Society of True-man" in his anthology, *When Love Comes around Us*, published in Seoul.

Why is man born into this world?
Who is a 'True-man'?
The desire to know these questions
Is met here accordingly.

Cause and effect (retribution),
Coexistence and co-prosperity,
Non-intervention,
Are the three rules of this universe?
Which we, blue minds, are to fulfill.

Many a blue mind has acquired these three
 Rules of the universe
And come here one by one
 To be a 'True-man'.

The True-men are the souls
Who have opened 'a posteriori world',
And regard the spirit of universe as their own.

They are the Deva Kings
Of the union of heaven, earth (nature), and human
beings,
And are together with the blessings
Of Heaven at all times.

All the True-men
Do bear in mind that for them, good things are good,
And bad things are
The key to the better things.

When asked by Mr. A to join his society of 'True-man', I told him to let me be a guest member to his society because I was living in a small local city far down from Seoul. Every time I went up to see him in his office, I would often meet some of his disciples easily, and we had a talk freely about strange psychic phenomena, and the future of Korea and the world as well. Some of the members seemed to practice hard to learn the skills of psychic research, following Mr. A.

As Mr. A worked formally as a natural treatment therapist in society, we often talked about a natural cure for all the chronic diseases. His 'AOM' vibrated water could be the probable remedy for all diseases, by driving out all the dirt stored within the human body.

On a cold wintry day afternoon, Mr. A talked about the three possible kinds of world crises, which might come around the end of the century.

Out of a sheer folly and wicked desire, a nuclear war would break out and in the end, be expanded into the Third World War.

Nostradamus had once predicted that a dreadful fire would fall from Heaven unto earth, there would be a terrible war in the world, and an incurable disease somewhat like the plague in the Middle Ages would follow this.

The great prophet, Nam, Sa-go, who had lived in Korea in the sixteenth century, when Nostradamus lived, had also foretold the coming end of this world around the end of the century. His famous prediction book, titled *Kyucam Yurok*-a hermit's message- written in the sixteenth century, now is very popular in Japan according to the press. He too had warned us about the approaching war on earth: "There would come down fire with a small head and no feet from heaven, turning this world into a swirling chaos and leaving few behind in this gloomy world."

The second disaster would be the dreadful one as St. K had once predicted early in the twentieth century, like other prophets as well: Around the end of twentieth century, a formidable disease would be prevalent to warn the wicked people.

Mr. A argued that St. K would be one of several souls comprising his mind; and his 'AOM' vibrated water could be the weapon of Heaven against the horrible disease due to prevail in the near future.

When he first heard of AIDS, he wondered if AIDS was the very malignant disease St. K had predicted. However, he said he could hardly be sure of himself, because he had not met an AIDS patient, or done any clinical examination of the disease. For Mr. A, proving his theory about curing AIDS through his 'AOM' water was necessary in order to make the public accept his idea.

One day, Mr. A introduced an opening episode, which sounded strange enough-a commutation with 'Gilmo', the AIDS virus, through his telepathic ability.

It was early in January 1986.

An attractive young woman, who had graduated from S university in Seoul, and gone to the United States for a Ph.D., once visited him with a gloomy face. She said she had to pass the written preliminary examination before writing the dissertation for her doctorate. However, she had failed in this important examination twice running, just missing zero for the same blank answer sheet, in spite of herself. Any sound-minded student would not commit such a mistake more than once. Wondering why she made such an unbelievable mistake twice, she guessed there could be some mysterious reason, or spiritual cause there, unexplained by common sense; and so, using the short-term break of the winter semester, she returned to Korea, and came to see Mr. A in the hope of solving her own strange problem.

She told Mr. A that she believed she could find the answer to the riddle by having a talk with him, because she had once read some of Mr. A's spiritual books.

However, the moment Mr. A met her, he received a strange communication about the unknown substance called AIDS, through telepathy. He could hardly believe the fact that the AIDS virus could be a life form intelligent enough to communicate with a human being like Mr. A, a physicist of spiritual ability, through telepathy. So, at first, Mr. A himself believed it was a kind of auditory hallucination; but the next moment, he was greatly surprised to learn the message through the medium of this young woman, was so logical and reasonable.

Mr. A said later that he might have a remedy for AIDS, using information acquired through telepathy with the substance called 'Gilmo'.

A few years ago, Mr. A said, he had visited the US twice to have a talk with an American scientist about how to get a cure for AIDS, having made a previous appointment. Yet disappointingly, the American scientist did not even try to listen to him.

"I'm sure AIDS will be cured by scientists within one or

two years. Go back to your country, as I do not need your help."

The scientist did not even see Mr. A for half an hour, which was rather rude, though they had made an appointment to talk with each other in advance. He had to go to the States twice from Korea, but they rejected him out of hand, almost regarding him as an insane person.

Mr. A thought that if Americans carried on with such an arrogant mentality, they faced the peril of their lives with the rapid spread of the AIDS virus. This was dumbfounding to him.

On his way back home, he confronted a fierce gangster with a gun in downtown Los Angeles, threatened with death on the spot, but made a narrow escape from the jaws of death.

The former white cowboys had killed about fifty million native Indians, and for that unpardonable sin, they would, Mr. A believed, perish in the end.

Mr. A was in an angry mood when he told us the reason he had gone to America.

"I went there to help them out with the AIDS problem, as they had helped our people a lot in the past, including the liberation of the Korean people from the Japanese colonialism, and in the Korean War too. Nevertheless, the American scientist did not want to talk with me, treating me as if I was a crazy person. Then why in the world did she make an appointment to meet me? Well, I tried my utmost, but I can't help any longer."

After a while, I asked him, "By the way, what do you think this fearful disease, which all the prophets have warned us about in the past would be like? If the disease were to spread by aerial infection, in the way flu is caught, I don't think there will be a remedy, or any escape from the inevitable termination of human race on earth, I'm afraid."

"Yes, almost every prophet in both East and West alike has warned us about this terrible disease. And I think if AIDS gets worse by becoming an airborne disease, there will be an end to all of us, though now it's believed to be infectious by blood and sperm only."

After a pause, he added, "Along with these two future crises-the possibility of nuclear war and horrible disease-the third crisis is the ever-increasing pollution of nature and air."

Of late, all our natural environments grow polluted to an unlimited degree around the world; this goes with the physical culture of the West to seek for sensual pleasure and bodily ease, under the nice-sounding name of development or civilization.

This trivial little speck of humankind seems completely ignorant of his insignificance, but is arrogant and uncontrollable, always going against nature or Heaven's will.

This earth is rapidly becoming a wasteland, or a troubled world, as Buddha calls it.

This damned animal, the human being, has been randomly destroying the natural environment until now, and has acted as if he was an omnipotent god or Prometheus, to our great regret.

Now, we human beings are living a life-in-death in this hellish world, and this is lamented by modern poets as well.

So can we avoid the final catastrophe?

CHAPTER 8
The Spirit of the Universe

Almost every time Mr. A met people, he used to talk often about the spirit of the universe: Cause and Effect (the law of retribution), Co-prosperity and Coexistence, and Non-intervention.

Of the three, the first and most important law of this vast universe is cause and effect, that is, the law of retribution.

As is well known, Buddha awakened all of a sudden after his long and hard mental practice, learning that the rule of cause and effect governs this vast universe.

The spirit of the universe is like a kind of vast computer. Everything we do, think and speak in our daily life, the spirit of the universe makes a record of it without fail, and accordingly, the result will come out eventually.

"As Edgar Cayce did, can you read the so-called 'Acashik Record' in Heaven?" I once asked Mr. A.

"Yes, I can. It is a great library in Heaven. Everything on earth, and all that we say, think, and act in everyday life, it is all recorded," he said in a sincere voice.

Some say that Edgar Cayce could read in his sleep the spiritual record in the psychic world called 'Acashik Record', the great heavenly library where all the information of what has passed or is to come on earth is stored.

Through the spiritual readings in his sleep, he could predict all the things to come in this world. In short, the recorded things are the program of all future things due to happen on earth.

Today's world is the world in which everyone follows the law of the jungle, leading all of us to the predetermined final annihilation. It is the world in which the Western culture prevails, the so-called 'a priori world' in Buddhism.

Maitreya rules began in May 1989, which is when the Oriental culture became overwhelmingly prevalent in that 'a posteriori world'. Henceforth all the people are going to get along well with each other in a mood of coexistence and co-prosperity.

Today's people have been accustomed to the law of jungle, mainly influenced by Western civilization, but they do not know what the future world of co-prosperity will be like. Therefore, Mr. A was eager to read the so-called spiritual record in the psychic heaven, whose contents are as follow:

(1) All the nations in Asia will merge into one.
(2) All the countries in Europe will unify in the near future.
(3) Northern and Southern America will unify, and Africa will form into one regional union.

The Asian regional union will be a role model for other peoples on earth, prompting them to build their own respective regional federations, which before long will become the final world joint union.

As T.S. Eliot tells us in his "The Waste Land", Mr. A said that man is to be born into this weary world with the previous 'memory(=karma)' stored up in his subconscious and personal 'desire'.

In this destined cycle of transmigration, the unavoidable law of retribution (cause and effect) will triumph unfailingly.

To Eliot, this world was a world with seas of troubles, as Buddha calls it, hoping eagerly to get away from it a.s.a.p. if he could. Lilac may be the symbol of reincarnation into this troubled world against one's free will; and April, the month for the rebirth into this prison-like world, may be the cruelest for that reason.

There are three seeds of karma: what we speak, think and act in daily life. They go into kind of great computer or black box in the psychic world, forming an absolute karma for the next transmigration, along with what we desire sincerely in our minds.

This is the fundamental theory of Buddhism or Hinduism, attested to be real by the modern psychic science or parapsychology.

After long and hard mental discipline, Buddha had

awakened and learned that the crucial law of retribution rules everything in the universe.

Supposedly, T.S. Eliot studied deeply about Hinduism and Buddhism for several years, and may have converted to Buddhism when he wrote "The Waste Land."

Mr. A said that his late father had always maltreated his poor wife in his lifetime, and strove hard not to die, hoping to live longer in this world; as a result, his father had been born again as a woman, his last daughter.

One day, Mr. A told me about a strange and interesting episode concerning his daughter, the reincarnation of his late father.

Mr. A's father passed away at the age of seventy.

Before he died, he had drunk to excess and often fallen ill over several decades. In a sense, he lived long, considering that he drank too much for so long. However, he hated the idea of leaving this world very much.

At that time, Mr. A had no psychic or supernatural power, and so he tried to make his father maintain a fast, in order to cure his liver cancer. His only maternal uncle, who was with him by the sickbed of his father, agreed to this; but his mother who was not there with them made a great fuss, saying that he was belittling her. She made an international telephone call to his brothers living in the States, charging him unjustly with starving his father to death out of greed and wanting to get all his fortune.

To be frank, it was the mother who wanted him die, not Mr. A. His parents had been on bad terms with each other for most of their lives. His mother told him coldly to get his father released from the S hospital just as his father's illness turned out to be liver cancer.

Mr. A, however, had a different idea about his father, even though he had lived with somewhat complicated feelings toward him; but wanted to be a good son to his father even in the worst situation, practicing filial piety toward his father, although he always used to curse him bitterly, saying to his first son, "You'll be nothing, I'm sure."

Therefore, he tried his utmost to save his father from illness.

On receiving an international phone call from their mother, all of his brothers returned to Seoul in great haste. They only believed in contemporary medical science, not listening to Mr. A at all.

His brothers insisted strongly that their father be hospitalized in the hospital of S university and be checked to see if he really had liver cancer. However, the herb doctors in the sanitarium for fast treatment told him not to have a check, worrying that it might worsen the improving condition of his father. Yet they ignored this advice, and made their father receive the check.

The result was quite an unexpected one.

The doctor said that they must have made a wrong diagnosis, because they could not find any progress of cancer in Mr. A's father after the first check, which was an extremely rare case, and hardly ever encountered.

There was a great fuss in his family. They falsely accused Mr. A of trying to starve his father to death.

Despite Mr. A's sincere advice, his father left the sanitarium, and after three days, he suddenly took a turn for the worse. It turned out to be true that he had a liver cancer.

Therefore, Mr. A sent his father to an asylum for fast treatment, but it was almost hopeless. The herbalists told him that it had been as fatal for his father to have the radioactivity check after the long fast treatment.

There was no use in their being sorry about it.

Before his father became unconscious, he reproached and cursed his first son, saying that he should have kept his brothers from sending him to the hospital for radioactivity examination, even if they wrongly accused him of the homicide of his father. Mr. A prayed earnestly to God to lengthen the lifespan of his father at the sacrifice of his own lifespan; but was in vain, and finally his father died.

From that day on, a serious problem arose.

Every night his father appeared in his dream, and urged Mr. A to make him come alive, and so Mr. A was almost near a nervous breakdown. He was practicing birth control at that time because he could not afford to have another child-only two, given the state of his family finances.

His father was buried in his grave, and no one can make the dead alive again in this world; but the only way to make him reborn was by spiritual means.

Mr. A consulted with his wife about this, and stopped using birth control.

"If my father is born again, he'll possibly be reborn on his first sacrifice day, when you'll bear him suddenly midway through preparing for the sacrifice; and he is likely to be born as a daughter, as he had maltreated my mother severely throughout his whole life," predicted Mr. A.

Before long, his wife had a dream of her forthcoming conception. She said she had visited her father-in-law's grave with her husband in her dream, but she saw through the grave and found the coffin quite empty. She was on her way back home with her father-in-law, and woke from the dream. Soon after that, she had a sign of her pregnancy, when she was aged forty.

As predicted by Mr. A, she was busily preparing the ritual food for her father-in-law, and had a sudden feeling that she would soon have a child. Therefore, she went to a hospital, and safely delivered a girl early on the morning of her father-in-law's ancestral rite. On hearing of her early labor, Mr. A ran quickly to the hospital, and found the newborn baby lying on her face beside his wife.

The moment when Mr. A told his wife, "You had a lot of trouble in your delivery. Please accept my congratulations!" the newborn child suddenly raised her head, and burst out crying.

"You son of a bitch, I wanted you to make me alive, but you have only reincarnated me as your daughter!"

His father's voice, trembling with wrath seemed to ring in his ears.

His last daughter looked just like his late father.

After his wife left the hospital, the new child slept at night between his wife and him. When he dreamed in the night, his late father lay asleep between them.

Frequently, his father (the baby) tried to communicate with him through telepathy.

After six months had passed, when she was past breast-feeding, his father's looks began to disappear from the baby's face. The communication through telepathy from his father stopped completely.

He had a real first-hand experience of the fact that man has a memory of his former life within six months of his birth.

We can say a man's soul is reborn in this world according to his karma in his previous life.

Mr. A believed firmly that his father could be born again in this world as his last daughter because his late father wanted to be alive again, and he desired to make him reborn as his daughter.

Hearing his rather strange and interesting story, I managed to understand the strict law of retribution in this vast universe, the heavenly secret concerning life and death in the universe.

They say, by the way, a man is rarely able to live his life calmly with sins in the depth of his unconscious.

As all the people have a prick of conscience in their minds, if a person commits a crime, and then not punished at all for it, he will punish himself unconsciously within the depth of his subconscious, that is, self-punishment.

Mr. A explained, "If a person commits a crime, but then not punished for the sin accordingly, he'll have a strong guilty feeling in his mind at all times. So, through his self-punishment, in one way or other, he'll come to be relieved of the painful guilty feeling," and then he added, "To get free of the guilt complex by punishing oneself, is a stark kind of proof that the law of retribution is being observed faithfully in the vastness of eternity, I believe."

All the white Americans were emigrants from their native countries in Europe, mostly from England, and considering themselves as the second or 'new' Adam in their minds, they ruthlessly massacred countless number of Native Americans. They were killers, these uninvited strangers, who killed and drove the host people out of their homeland. The bloody whites had tried to build another 'Adam's Eden' or 'the Promised Land' on the new American continent.

They had been outlaws or yahoos, in a sense, committing unpardonable sins, and thus formed mountain-high karmas stored in the deep heart of universe, called the 'Acashik Record'. In the spirit of the universe, karma works strictly according to the law of retribution, with no exception.

Besides the massacre of the Indian tribes, the white cowboys maltreated the black people as their poor slaves, inflicting all kinds of ills and misdeeds on them.

According to a psychical scientist like Mr. A, if a man with a heavy karma in his previous life is born into this world, he'll have to suffer from the piled-up bitterness of life, especially human suffering in the course of life.

A Buddhist monk or psychic therapist will stipulate almost with the same voice the strict realization of the law of retribution on earth according to the previous karma.

Mr. A had once said, "There are two kinds of ways to be freed from the karma piled in a former life: one is suffering according to the law of retribution, and the other is love. In short, a man born into this world who has shouldered a heavy karma seems to muddle through the hardest difficulties in life, even doing good things to others as well. That would be a way to expiate from the former karma or sins earlier than he expects."

We must suffer from lots of painful bitterness according to the rule of retribution in this vast universe, but if we love other people and do good to them, our karma will be cleaned out much earlier to that extent; besides making a way through suffering.

I firmly believe there has seemed to exist a deep-seated guilty feeling stored down in the hearts of American whites for their ancestors' formidable sins committed in the past: the unbelievable slaughter of the Indian tribes, and making slaves of imported black people from Africa.

Another regret lying in their hearts may be the sense of escape or exodus from their own fatherland to an unknown continent.

These two kinds of negative feelings have until now been the constant motifs or central ideas in their writings.

As a kind of mental compensation, frequently we find the appearance of an inappropriate love or friendship between two people of the same sex but different races, mostly between white and black or Indian. For example, in Mark Twain's *The Adventures of Huckleberry Finn*, we find a sincere affection between two young people of the same sex, white Huck and black Jim.

There is also a recurring motif of strangers escaped from their home country or parents. Unlike the British novel, in which a wandering person returns to his father in the end, as the prodigal son did in the Bible, the American cowboy frequently runs away from his father or home, as did his Pilgrim Fathers in the bygone days; he is the second or 'new' Adam looking for another paradise on the vast continent.

This deep-felt idea shows up as the spirit of the frontier, searching for an unknown place toward the West, with the settled places left behind; it is a lonely and courageous concept.

Unlike the Japanese people, who have been the bad neighbor to the countries nearby throughout their long history, the American cowboys have done good things for many other nations, compared with other countries.

With their archetypal outlook of awe of anybody superior, the cunning and shrewd Japanese samurai people are always humble before the strong, but arrogant before the weak.

They fall to their knees eagerly before anyone strong or powerful, learning what they can from him, and then are ready to betray their benevolent helper or teacher at the next instant-thus, returning evil for kindness at all times.

Their lasting national slogan has been, 'To let every nation take its proper station', under the eight-poled roof of the world, ruled by their own emperor on top. With this unchangeable motto, the samurai people declared war on America, launching a surprise attack on their teacher and helper, the cowboy people. The Japanese national cycle is like a treacherous wave-'To use and then betray'.

They always try to take advantage of everyone around them fully, but if they no longer find him of any use, they turn a cold shoulder on him all of a sudden, and then, betray him, returning evil for good at all times.

They always despise the weak openly before their eyes, and then, trying to conquer them by force, after using them.

I think both the cowboy, or gunman and the samurai, or swordsman, are almost the same in their natures, in that the two peoples both have endless expansionism. The cowboy has the 'Manifest Destiny' to rule and lead all the nations on earth, and samurai 'the eight-poled roof of the world' with his emperor on top, under which the samurai lets every nation take its proper station.

They said that cowboy had fought with two enemies from inside and outside the nation. From outside the nation, cowboy fought against the communist Soviet Union, and within the nation, he fought with Japan in a trade war.

In the cold war, the American cowboy finally beat the Soviet Union late in 1980s after the sudden unexpected collapse of communist countries. Only a very few remain.

Yet the cowboy suffered greatly in the economic war against the samurai, as the cowboy placed the highest emphasis upon the national security, performing the role of the world police for the free world.

While the cowboy fought desperately with the communists, samurai was using him to the full, exporting Japanese goods to flood the American markets.

The egocentric samurai has used the cowboy fully, and grown to be haughty and treacherous, as before.

The cowboy has been kind, frank and somewhat naive.

He had fought against the reds in Korea, Vietnam and other troublesome places as well, acting as if he were the world's police.

Of course, the cowboy has done many good things for other poor people on earth, and spread the concept of American democracy until now, with the idea of Christian love; but his ancestors had committed too many formidable sins or karmas to do enjoy forgiveness.

CHAPTER 9
The Coming Evils

Ralph W. Emerson seems influenced by William Wordsworth during his stay in Europe, and his disciple, Thoreau, chose to live in seclusion in the woods. His philosophy of transcendentalism looks somewhat like Chinese natural philosophy, that is, Taoism, in a sense.

However, to my mind, the USA, Adam's second or new land, has become the place of materialism and mammon. It has lost its naive and fresh ideal, 'American dream', and is wildly addicted to sex, alcohol, drugs, violence and brutal crimes, including murder and rape; and then there is AIDS.

Today, American culture has taken a leading role in Western culture. Some say that American culture is a 'rotten culture', which only looks for sensory pleasure, and the lowbrow satisfaction of physical desires.

When I traveled around the big cities, what I saw could be the very symbol of American vice and tragedy. Burnt-out and dilapidated buildings stood in ruins, scattered around the hearts of the cities.

Rabbit-eyed drunkards strolled about city centers, crying aloud, "Hey! Give me money, okay?"

This great and vast country is now becoming the center

of human vices and wicked animalism, I am afraid.

When I was in the States, I often asked myself. Is this the reality of Adam's new paradise, which the cowboys have built for themselves?

In Florida, I once talked with Dr. N, a professor in the English Department, about the reason most Americans are allowed to carry guns with them, and how come the big cities have come to be 'killing fields', like Detroit, for example.

The white professor deplored this, "Yes, it's our shame, the shame of America," he said.

It seems that the fine ideal of the cowboy-'American dream'-has gone, having lost its meaning. There is no value in his life, immersed, as it is in the dirty and vulgar culture of sex and money-oriented life-style, that is, a living death in the midst of life, as portrayed in Hemingway's novels.

Well, in its outward appearance, this huge and vast cowboy country was 'a place in the sun', blessed with God's favor: the vast continent, the enormous amount of natural resources, the kind-hearted people, the attractive, well-made females, and the forest-covered land with its picturesque, awe-inspiring beauty...

However, the problem is, for all the God's blessings, this vast country seems to have now come to be a pit of human vices and misery.

One of the Oriental students would often ask, "What in

the world is the Federal Government for, if it's not even maintaining public security in the cities?"

When I was young, we kids all regarded this cowboy country as kind of 'the land of paradise' or 'Adam's new Eden' we most wanted to go and live in.

The 'Made in USA' label was the symbol of the best quality in the whole world, and American GIs seemed to be the kind-hearted friends of all of us. Truly, 'American style' was the popular symbol of fashion, beauty and high quality.

The early pilgrims came over to the new continent with the ultimate dream of building Adam's new paradise on the American continent, thinking themselves as would-be 'reincarnated Adams'.

Now, this vast cowboy country seems to have become sort of a land of AIDS, formidable violence and crime, the degraded morality of carnal desire, alcoholism, and drugs. Losing almost its greenish tinge of a dream and swayed by a corrupted Yankee culture of money-oriented social mechanism, the US is shortsighted by vulgar physical desire, just as Rome experienced before its downfall.

We would often ask, "Has this vast continent become a stage where cowboys fight each other with guns as in the Western cowboy movies?"

The cowboy movies looked romantic, however, arousing a vague longing for nature; like the films, Clint Eastwood appeared in as a hero, with a cigar set casually in his mouth and a gun at his waist, when I was a college student in the 1960s.

This cowboy country appears to have turned into a place of vice and evil, and even 'killing fields' in the big cities.

All the prophets in both East and West alike, along with the Bible, have warned us strongly about the forthcoming disasters we human beings will suffer around the end of century.

They are Nostradamus, Edgar Cayce, and G.M. Scallion, who is a computer scientist now living in the States; many other Oriental prophets, including Nam, Sa-go, called the Korean Nostradamus who also lived in the sixteenth century; and St. K in the early twentieth century.

They have predicted a terrible war, possibly the Third World War, a horrible epidemic disease, and environmental pollution of air and water, plus a sudden shift in the earth's axis, causing violent movements including volcanoes, earthquakes, and even the sinking and rising of continents.

Now is the time capitalism prevails almost all over the world, following the sudden collapse of communist countries, leaving only a few, including the closed North Korea and Cuba.

As capitalism is by nature reliant upon a human being's individual egoism, it may be easily linked with materialism and mammon and the will to power, besides causing wars, corruption, keen competition, the disorientation of modern man, and degraded morality, arousing almost every variety of vice and evil on earth.

As is well known, the USA has been the real center for all of these cultural features and Western civilization.

Certainly, more than a few people have foretold the coming fall of capitalism in the next century, and suggested its replacement by Oriental thought instead.

They say that peaceful harmony between man and nature, or between people and people, will be widely prevalent on earth in the bright twenty-first century if we human beings could survive the catastrophe foretold around the end of the century. Then the Oriental philosophy of harmony between man and nature, and coexistence between man and man, will prevail in the days to come.

Well, we human beings should strive to live with good-natured hearts in order to survive the ordeals predicted around the turn of the century. We should help other people as if we were the same flesh and blood in daily life, because we are all the children of the Maker from the view of psychic science, and we share a bit of His divine nature, deep within each of our hearts, called 'Over Soul' by Emerson.

Among many famous predictors, the sleeping prophet, Edgar Cayce, and the contemporary scientist, G.M.

Scallion, are two typical American seers concerning the future of their own country, the USA.

Last year, on an autumn day, I went up to Seoul to see Mr. A as I had no class that day.

There were some members of his society and many other visitors in the waiting room, sitting and talking with each other.

After Mr. A talked with lots of visitors from around the country in turn, we began to have a free conversation about various topics; his wife served us coffee and a soft drink.

Over a cup of coffee, we talked about the future of the Korean peninsula, and then about the predictions concerning the future of the world including those of Japan and the USA.

We were most worried about the horrible epidemic about to spread by aerial infection in the near future to come.

Mr. J, a journalist in Seoul, asked Mr. A, "What do you think would be a remedy for the impending critical airborne disease at this time?"

Dr. Kim added, "Our past predictors like Nam, Sa-go, and St. K, predicted that a horrible epidemic would happen without fail, to answer for the piled karmas that wicked human beings had made for so long in human history. And if that disaster is unavoidable to us in the near future, is there no way out of it, anywhere in the world?"

"Well, many famous prophets have made almost matching kinds of predictions about the future of the world-the same except on a very few points. They have also warned us to live with good-natured hearts, helping each other, and loving nature as well, in good harmony with people and the environment, instead of aggression, hatred and destruction. In short, we human beings should live as good and kind-hearted people, and not be wicked and ill natured as the Japanese people have been. In that sense, Buddha and Jesus are almost same in their emphasis on mercy and love respectively. We should live with mercy or love towards others, and respect nature with piety just like William Wordsworth, instead of arrogant conquest or destruction of it," said Mr. A heartily.

"Let me see," said I, "I have studied Oriental thoughts and tactical strategy for a long time. But every time I ponder about the law of coexistence and co-prosperity in the 'Spiritus Mundi', the spirit of the universe, I always feel kind of conflict in my mind. As we know well, the law of jungle, that is, the world of natural aggression, rules this world. We are living in the world in which we 'Conquer (win), or we are conquered (defeated)!" as Napoleon said. This world is in sharp contrast with that world (Heaven) as a way of living. Very contrasting I think. So, people have doubted about even the existence of the Creator

Himself, or wondered if He might not be good in His nature, hoping He would side with good person in every matter as a kind of judge between right and wrong. Well, I think only Confucius believed this, but everything looks the opposite of what we think it ought to be!"

"Well, the a priori world is gone already, and now is in a posteriori world, one of coexistence and co-prosperity. I believe the past a priori world was the era in which Western thought prevailed, but the Oriental philosophy of coexistence will govern this a posteriori world," Mr. A said confidently.

"By the way, what will Japan and the USA be like in the future?" Ms. L asked suddenly. She was a serene woman, and worked for a publisher in Seoul.

Then Mr. A answered in a serious voice. "According to Edgar Cayce, strong earthquakes will occur and volcanoes explode along the coastline in California and in some of the Southern states, and in the East in New York City. The upheavals will come first and then frightening floods, and then those parts would sink down into the sea. The ancient, lost continents of Atlantis and Mu will rise above the Atlantic Ocean. There may be a shift of the earth's axis. These things will mostly happen around the end of twentieth century..."

"The leading American prophet seems to be Scallion, who is a scientist living now in the States. They say he predicted the horrible earthquakes in Los Angeles (1992), and Kobe in Japan (1995), and some other volcanic explosions as well. His warnings sound almost like those of Cayce, but a very few. Among several dreadful things, he argued that the explosion of Mt. Rainier in Washington would be the start of the fall of America. Major parts of America, especially California, would sink into the sea, and then America would be divided, and turned into chaos," Dr. Kim said.

"Edgar Cayce seems to have predicted the sinking of Japan and America in his sleep. Japan will go into the sea, and large parts of America would also sink," he added again.

"I say, this will be an unavoidable fate for both the samurai and cowboy people in the near future. The two peoples have before now a mountainous heap of bad karma and this is a world ruled by the strict law of retribution," an aged Buddhist monk said calmly and then added.

"There seems to be no choice for the Japanese people, as they have lived as wicked and ill-natured as they were before, not feeling guilty or regretful at all for their past vices and misdoings towards innocent nations. However, the cowboys have tried to do good things a lot to the people who are in need on earth, and acted would-be 'world police' to preserve freedom against communists. But their ancestors had committed too many a mountain of bad karma in the past, I'm afraid."

However, the next moment, Mr. A continued in a sincere voice, "Well, the most important thing you should realize is the fact that we human beings are to know the reality of future to come. Of course, we can say there will be the psychic record called 'Acashik Record' in Heaven, which may be a programmed schedule for the future.

However, the important thing to note is that it may be changeable, and so, the future could be flexible to a certain degree. If we live good-naturedly, helping each other and in good harmony with people and nature (as the Oriental thought teaches us to do), with a positive view of the future in our hearts, the accumulated karmas will be lessened little by little; and so the predicted tragedy may be alleviated and offset."

The Oriental thought has as its basic idea that man is a part of nature, belonging in the bosom of his natural milieu, which is the embodiment of Heavenly will, or the spirit of the universe, just like the thinking of Wordsworth and Emerson.

Most prophets have said that around the turn of century the ordained punishment of Heaven will come for the wicked and wretched human animals.

To survive the coming catastrophe, man should live an honest and warm-hearted life, doing good deeds to others and following the spirit of 'coexistence and co-prosperity' of the universe.

As said by seers almost with one voice, predictions are to be flexible in time to occur; but they may be sure to happen eventually than we expect, to our greatest worry.

The commonest thought among the Oriental people is, 'He who goes against Heaven's dictates shall perish.'

CHAPTER 10
The Star-Spangled Banner

South Korea was the only country in the world where, "Yankee Go Home!" was foreign among Koreans, until early in the 1980s. However, the anti-US sentiment appears to have been on the increase in Korea from around the end of 2002, to our great regret.

In June 2002, during the heated period of World Cup event in Korea, an unhappy accident happened reportedly in a city near by Seoul that two Korean middle school girl students died on the road, killed by an armored car driven by the American GIs who were under the military training at that time.

At first, it seemed that most of the Korean people did not have it at heart seriously, just regarded it as one of unhappy accidents occurred in the military operation. Nevertheless, late in the fall, the accident came to awaken a sudden interest among the Korean nationals, when a jury found the two American soldiers 'not guilty' and acquitted them freely; and they departed for their country the next day.

Well, hardly knowing of the American legal system, some Korean people may have felt kind of sorrow within their hearts as the people of one of small countries.

Meanwhile, quite contrary to our first expectation, in spite of a great deal of various helping supplies sent to North from South for several years, the North communist regime has often threatened South with a wild military card, instead of 'thank-you' note; and on and off, waged armed provocations against South Korea repeatedly. In addition, for the worse, it turned out that the North Korea has continued to develop the nuclear weapons secretly against the international agreements; and in these days, the North regime has begun to say openly that it has A-bombs indeed.

Then, is it true that the North Korean communist regime has now discarded its chronic plot to communize South Korea, and is trying to get along well with South for common prosperity with the so-called love of same Korean native race at its heart?

North Korea is now threatening to attack Japan, and even the US, the sole world super-power, with its self-developed nuclear weapons any time if it wants, while in South Korea, the blood alliance between Korea and the US for more than 50 years is almost verging on break-up worriedly enough.

Faced with this on-going national danger, several hundred-thousand people gathered voluntarily. From across the country in Korea on the wide plaza of the City Hall in Seoul on the last anniversary of independence movement under the Japanese colonial reign in March, that of outbreak of the Korean War in June, and that of Korean liberation from the Japanese cruel colonialism in August, respectively.

Every one of them was holding two national flags of Korea and the US in his or her hands altogether. They shouted at the top of their voices, "Remember the Korean War, Down with Kim, Jong-il!" and waved their hearty thanks for America in those national rallies against the North Korean regime.

All the attendants on the wide city plaza sang the Korean and the American national anthem loudly, waving high two national flags in their both hands. In the clear open sky, the three super sized flags of Korea, America, and the United Nations were streaming in the blowing wind.

They prayed for the American victory in its war on the terrorism, and wished President Bush good luck.

It seems that the majority of Korean people think Mr. George W. Bush, the confident cowboy-like conservative who is full of go, has been dealing with the knotty North Korean nuclear bomb problem wisely in a determined manner. Well, now, America is no longer a 'paper tiger' in the bygone days as the late Chinese communist Chairman Mao used to call scornfully.

Reportedly, as he openly proclaimed, President Bush

may be called another Mr. Reagan, who made it possible for the depressed cowboy people regain the self-confidence in themselves and Americanism itself, pulling themselves out of the swamp of the 'Vietnam syndrome'.

With his slogan of the 'Great America', the king-like President Reagan tided the cowboy people over the chronic crisis of confidence, thus getting them to feel the 'Old Glory' of America once again at their hearts, as signified by their national emblem of the Stars and Stripes.

Mr. Reagan was a great leader as well as a great communicator, who made his people recover their confidence in their ability and pride in their country once again. That was just possible through Mr. Reagan's leadership for the 'spiritual rise' of American cowboy people, which enabled them overcome the national crisis, and become the final victor in the cold war with the Soviet Union.

Truly, like his predecessor, President George W. Bush has won the 'war against terrorism' successively in Afghanistan and Iraq since the unexampled shock and awe of 9/11 occurred in 2001.

It seems that now is the right time for Kim, Jong-il to awake from his nightmare. His wicked plot to make South Korea another Vietnam in vain, and give up nukes, and other weapons of mass destruction once and for all; and instead, he should try all that he can do to feed his starving people, and let them live in peace as a human being. That can be a way for him to survive, and to atone for his piled-up sins.

In the mid-nineties, I wrote an English book, titled *Cowboy and Samurai* viewed by the ancient Chinese tactical strategy called 'Sunz tactics'; it was written with a view to comparing the two sharply-opposing peoples with each other, largely centered on each of their archetypal patterns and national cycles.

This book is in the Library of Congress registered there through my agent in the US; but it was not published in the States to my regret.

Last summer, I wrote a paper on the reality of American cowboy; and it is in the collection of papers published by the university press.

Last week, I happened to talk about the American leadership for the world peace with a few college teachers and writers in this local city; we had a free talk in the conference room at my 'Chongpa (blue waves)' Office for the literary research. My wife served green tea and coffee for us. Unexpectedly, the meeting lasted more than two hours in a sincere mood.

Dr. Lee, a professor of politics, said it first, "The American capture of Saddam Hussein on December 13 is likely to be a turning point of President Bush's war on terrorism in the Middle East regions, especially in Iraq." After a pause awhile, he continued, "Few people may have expected before that Saddam got captured like that; he looked so mean and unmanly when American soldiers tried to get him in a spider hole. He did not even dare to kill himself, unlike a former dictator who had survived by iron-fisted ruthlessness."

"Well, in the wake of Saddam's capture, it seems that the light is on for 'Go' for Mr. Bush. Since he declared the official termination of war in Iraq on May 1, the American GIs, along with other allied forces have fought a bitter battle against the pro-Saddam's surviving Iraqi forces for more than half a year, and took a heavy toll of about two hundred American war dead. For the worse, the so-called anti-war doves, just like wildfire around the world, have spread the massive antiwar movements. But, Mr. Bush is a real cowboy with plenty of guts just like his real political model, Mr. Reagan," said Dr. Yim sincerely, who teaches history at G university.

"The American economy is picking up these days; and it is reported that the American public opinion is rising in favor of Mr. Bush in these days. Now he seems to feel assured that he will get his next target, Osama Bin Laden shortly; and then, he will be able to win the on-going hard-fought warfare against terrorism in the end. If his war plan is to be done as expected, I think every situation will be of advantage to Mr. Bush for his presidential re-election campaign in 2004," said I.

Outside the window, snowflakes began to flutter in the air. Then the snow grew to dance and whirl in the wind. Soon it was snowing thick and fast in great flakes.

Over coffee or green tea, we looked up into the dark-clouded sky for a while. It was the first snow of this year. Just like kids, we often feel cheerful and even elevated in minds at the sight of first snowfall every year. It often carries our minds back to those days in our youth.

"By the way, what do you think the current American situation is like, Mr. Park? I heard that you've been to America recently, right?" I asked him smilingly. He is a novelist, and now works for a local press in this city.

"Yes, I've been to, a month before. Well, in a word, America may have made a complete about-face in its course of life from what it used to be after the unbelievable shock of 9/11 attacks in 2001.

"As is well known, after the US had won the cold war with communist countries, America voiced the 'Pax Americana' openly, where liberty and American democracy could prevail in the established order of global stage. Yet, unthinkably, unseen enemies within and without the cowboy country made surprise terror raids on the spirit buildings in New York City and Washington, D.C., simultaneously, using the innocent passengers and airplanes as involuntary suicide bombs and missiles.

Moreover, this unpardonable terrorism gave the cowboy people unforgettable shocks at the bottom of their hearts. Faced with the national danger, since 9/11 occurred, the US has built up its military strength to its fullest; and now no country can match America militarily. America has now become the sole world superpower unrivaled by any other country around the world.

"And contrary to the first negative view that the US might be bogged down in another swamp of Vietnam, Mr. Bush could win the war on terrorism with ease one after another in Afghanistan and Iraq with its ultra-modern science and weapons, which looked almost sort of computer games rather than regular wars. And now it can be safely said that no country can rival the US in a regular warfare with any other than bushwhacking or terrorism," stopped Mr. Park awhile.

"Did you go to the States last month to cover the 2nd anniversary of 9/11 attacks?" asked Ms. Kang with a curious look. Ms. Kang is an unmarried woman in her thirties; she is an essayist, majoring in Korean literature at a graduate school in Seoul.

"Yes, I was told to do news gathering for the changed face of American people after that terrible attacks as a legman. I went around seeing New York City and Washington, D.C.; and seeing with my own eyes the 'Ground Zero', the very site of WTC twin buildings," said Mr. Park, and then continued.

"Well, I can say that America is in the state of kind of mental swirl, and on the alert for the probable terrorist attacks from within and without the country. Everywhere you go in the States, the fiery patriotism is riding on the streaming waves of the Star-Spangled Banner. Stood America united! I say, and the sea of flying flags is rising in great waves on the vast American continent. Well, they are at war now with unseen enemies. Any other words or slogans, it seems, take a backseat to such words as 'anti-terrorism', 'patriotism, and 'unity' in their course of daily life."

"I think America is a country of stars. During my graduate study in the States, I tried to see things American with my own eyes as much as possible. Therefore, using the short quarter break for about a week, I once crossed over the vast continent from Washington, D.C. to San Francisco; and I went around across the country largely by Greyhound bus. While the bus was running fast, the American national anthem, 'the Star-Spangled Banner', was also traveling in the waves of soundtrack within the bus. It was very impressive to me at that time. The national song of stars and the national banner of stars were equally impressive. Well, I believe American cowboy people love stars, and stars are the symbol of their fervent love of America. Just as white cloud was a symbol of Hermann

Hesse for his ideal, so star is the emblem of American cowboy for American dream, like 'the lone star state' for the alias of Texas," said I, reflecting on the past days.

"It appears to us that Americans live along in the waves of the Stars and the Stripes in their daily life. Wherever you go in the States, the flags are flying freely in the air over all kinds of buildings including universities, schools, supermarkets, and even hamburger shops, not to mention the official government or public buildings. Not a few persons, young and old alike, like to wear clothes or hats with the design of their national banner; and they drive cars with the painting of the national flag on them," said Mrs. Kim, a poet.

"They say the full vigor or strength of the USA comes from the cowboy people's love of their country, and trust in their government as well witnessed in their unceasing, fervent love for their national banner, the Stars and the Stripes.

"When a child enters a kindergarten or pre-school, the first thing it learns is the oath of national flag, swearing the loyalty and freedom before the Stars and the Stripes as a citizen of the United States of America. It seems they take their national flag almost to a symbol of religion, loving and vowing the loyalty to the country completely, with the convinced belief that the USA government would keep them alive surely enough, as long as they do not forget the Stars and the Stripes.

"The great Star-Spangled Banner floating high in the wind over the top of every building across the country can be said to be the pride and confidence in their country stored deeply in their minds with the mentality of the so-called 'Manifest Destiny'," said I calmly, and then added again.

"Just as Alexander the Great had built the temple of Zeus on every land he conquered as the sign of expanded Grecian culture, so cowboys have carried along their flags with them wherever they have been over the world. They have a great pride in the slogan, 'Americanism No. 1'; and the Stars and Stripes are the symbol of their pride and patriotism as well as their frontier-based expansionism."

As is widely reported in the press, the American government has always shown its earnest love for its nationals from the past under any circumstance. For an instance, it did not hesitate to order its Six Fleet to move out into the Yugoslavian battle area, just to rescue a shot-down pilot unto it.

Moreover, even now, after the elapse of more than fifty years after the close of Korean War, the American government has been trying in earnest to gather even the ashes of war dead killed in North Korea during the war at the expense of great amount of dollars.

A few years ago, there occurred a shocking case of

killing with gun in the Capitol by an insane person, and lots of innocent persons including two cops, fell dead on the spot.

At this critical moment, not a few congressional representatives rushed into the most dangerous scene with no slight hesitation, and led people to safer places just before the firing muzzle of crazy gun.

Most of American leaders have always behaved themselves as the good example of their people; and both the government and the people do never forget the brave deeds of those who have sacrificed for their country. In a sense, they tend to make a hero of common persons who have died for the sake of their country. In addition, we saw their reality vividly on the actual spot of the unthinkable 9/11 attacks.

With the white-haired eagle's slogan, 'Unity in Diversity' or 'Diversity in Unity' in mind, American cowboy people work with diversified creativity, and unified harmony among themselves in every difficulty or crisis. In addition, this code of life, and love of their country consists of the good 'fundamentals' of the USA, the strong foundation of American force and order, that is, Pax Americana.

"What do you think about the fervent patriotism Americans have in mind for their country, Dr. Yi? I know you majored in American studies in the US for a doctorate, right?" I asked.

"Yes, you are right, Dr. Hahn. I studied American studies in Michigan for a Ph.D. about ten years ago. Well, let me see... in a sense, patriotism seems to have been sort of religion to every American citizen; and the Star-Spangled Banner is the name of their national flag and that of their national anthem at the same time. Their patriotism has been riding on the streaming waves of flying flags and sounding national songs. In short, the Star-Spangled Banner is the representation of American hearts and minds, I can say. They have an endless love for the United States of America from the bottom of their hearts, and trust in their government and political leaders. This can be called the real origin of their warm-hearted patriotism for their country as Walt Whitman sang aloud in his *Leaves of Grass*."

"Could you tell us about the so-called 'Manifest Destiny' Americans have in mind, Dr. Yi?" I asked him again.

"Sure, I will. The builders of America thought that it would be the responsibility of America to make world peaceful, in order, and still more, Americanized in every way. In other words, they thought that just as God created man in His shape, so America led the construct of nations in the world in its appearance. Most of American people have thought and acted with this kind of responsibility in mind to lead and rule all other peoples and nations with different ideas and values from those of American people, making them follow the American truth and justice. John Adams said in 1765 just before the independence of America from England that the founding of America was from the God's Providence to enlighten and free some of human beings on earth under the status of slavery. Well, America started to expand its land from buying Louisiana from France, and could annex California, Arizona, Nevada, Utah, and Colorado under its reign after the war with Mexico in 1847, the most brilliant victory ever since it began to enlarge its territory with the means of force and money, I think. This kind of ceaseless expansion of America has been due to the strong frontier, pioneering spirit of immigrants and their following generations, who migrated to new America, searching for freedom and equality. In addition, the national flag of America represents its history of expansion clearly, showing the steady process of adding stars on it for its history of two hundred years or so."

"Thank you, Dr. Yi. I know well what you are saying; and would you please tell us about 'American dream' especially in American literature?" I asked again.

"Well, we often use the term of 'American dream' to say about the essence of American culture or things American. In short, the American dream is the total sum of American ideal, including all kinds of positive aspects of American culture, and things American. In a wide sense of meaning, it means the dream of American democracy, of freedom and equality, and of new Adam's land. In a narrow sense, it means the social success, including the grasp of wealth and rise of social status, which everyone can achieve in the American society with no distinction of social station and economic ability as a self-made man, only through the virtues of diligence, honesty, perseverance, thrift, and devoutness. Closely related with the American dream is the frontiership, with which the first early settlers could have the endless hope for the possible potentiality on the free land as free people. This hope and belief for the infinite possibility of the free vast land was the basis of dream of American people. The American dream is a myth of new possibility of paradise, that is, the dream of Eden and myth of Adam's hero. The American opportunity and American equality, these anticipate the bright possibility for the future and American values."

"And then who was the first pathfinder of American dream to early settlers?" my wife cut in unexpectedly, who is deeply interested in history.

"Well, Benjamin Franklin, one of founding fathers, had once emphasized the usefulness of diligence and thrift to be wealthy to the early settlers. This was his teaching that 'To earn lots of money is the thing which is right and good morally.' This is the mental root of American people and basic idea of American dream, forming a part of Americanism. In a word, the life career of Benjamin

Franklin is the same road the newly born America has taken. The free, keen competition in the American society is possibly due to the social Darwinism of struggle for life, which emphasizes the survival of the fittest in the law of jungle. As the American dream puts a heavy stress upon the meaning of individualism and self-made man, the firm thought that everyone is the master of his own fate is deeply rooted into the hearts of American people as the sincere value of independence. The American dream is the dream that everyone can become a giant of millionaire by his own master of fate; this infinite expansion of self-enlightenment has enabled America to be what it is today.

"American writers have dealt with American dream as a major theme in their works, mostly with its tragedy as in *The Rise of Silas Lapham* by W.D.Howells, *Sister Carrie*, and *An American Tragedy* by T. Dreiser, and *The Great Gatsby* by F. Scott Fitzgerald."

"I know what you mean, but what is the tragedy of American dream?" My wife asked again in wonder.

"Well, the American dream has two kinds of meanings, those spiritual and physical or material at the same time; but, in the course of life, the mental or spiritual meaning vanished, and the physical one, especially material one has been rampant, raging in all its fury in the American society. This lack of spiritual meaning in the American dream seems to have resulted in the present materialism and pursuit of mammon in the States. At first, the American dream operates on the puritanical value and morality in itself, but its spiritual meaning was almost gone, leaving behind the physical culture of America only, running wild for money and sensual pleasure. This loss of spiritual meaning and morality in the American dream has resulted in the negative American syndrome, producing various social violence, crimes and evils in the American society."

"Would you kindly explain about the expansion and weakening of Americanism in American history?" asked Ms. Kang in her soft voice. "I think Americanism is the fervent desire for the ever-increasing expansionism in every aspect; it is based on a frontier attitude. Well, the American dream is the dream of American individual 'self-made man' who is nothing but free, independent-minded pioneer with the spirit of frontier attitude. This spirit of the frontier is the mind to seek things new and unknown, which has consisted of American consciousness. The American cowboy is the typical image of this pioneering frontier, which used to run across the vast land, searching for cows with the American dream in mind," he sipped his coffee and continued.

"Pax Americana is the world order or peace under the rule of Americanism, which is based on the somewhat romantic, free and liberal cowboy's dream of the frontier. The archetype of American cowboy can be the frontier spirit, 'Go ahead!' seeking things or lands new and unknown; and he is always on the move. This expansionism based on a frontier attitude has made it possible for American cowboy to establish the world order by Americanism as what it is today. When this pioneering mentality spreads everywhere to the outer world, it has often born good fruits, and the world order of Pax Americana. However, the ever-increasing expansionism based on pioneering spirit is baffled, and becomes internalized; it has resulted in all kinds of unhappy, pathological features of American people and society, such as drug, violence, formidable crimes, degradation of social morality, and even AIDS. Of all the serious problems in the American society, the loss of self-confidence, that is, the crisis of confidence called the 'Vietnam syndrome' may have been the most serious and knotty one to solve. It made this great young republic reel wildly in every field such as economy, culture, and even military affairs, by the heavy blows in and outside the nation. Faced with this urgent national crisis, the king President Mr. Reagan exerted his utmost to make the great America once again, and succeeded in building-up the strongest military forces in the world. Truly, he helped Americans recover the pride and confidence in their ability and American culture and value once again, realizing the actual reality of great America."

"By the way, I was greatly impressed by a surprise visit President Bush made to Baghdad at the risk of his life to have Thanksgiving dinner with his soldiers. That was a really great sight," said Mrs. Kim, a poet, in a somewhat excited voice, whose only son was in the front line as a Korean private soldier against the North Korean red army.

"Yes, you're right. I too felt deeply stirred by his surprising act of bravery for his dear life; no one expected him to go there for himself in the world. He must have caused the American public to gasp with surprise, I believe. Really, the news gave me a start. The current president of the United States of America dared any danger in Baghdad to cheer up his troop, and to see for him what was going on there," my wife chimed in with the poetess; her son too served his military duty at a Korean combatant police unit near by the front line.

"Well, I can say that's one of the real faces of the American political leaders. Mostly, general American people tend to trust in them, and rely on their country; and their warm-hearted patriotism, I think, comes from that deep-rooted confidence of their leaders and country. Even the Democrats, who assumed a critical attitude toward Mr. Bush's war policy in Iraq, said with one voice that his secret visit to Baghdad was great. That was the true reality of

American people, that is, the so-called 'Unity in Diversity', the unique motto Americans keep in their course of life. In every difficulty or national crisis, it seems, there is no distinction of the Republicans, and the Democrats among the people in the US, but exists only the 'American party', saying that they are all Americans," explained Dr. Yun, a scholar of foreign affairs.

"Dr. Yim, what about the so-called 'pre-crime system' the American neo-conservatives suggested for the preventive war, including the preemptive strike?" I asked sincerely.

"They say President Bush is a unilateralist cowboy or a typical, trigger-happy warmonger, which has been raised largely in the anti-war campaigns across the world. I think he is far from being a warmonger or neo-cons, even though he seems to have been influenced by them near around him. In a sense, it seems to us almost quite natural that Mr. Bush should step up efforts to launch a retaliatory strike in the aftermath of the lethal terrorist assaults on the spirit buildings in two iconic cities. Faced with the biggest test as the president of the United States of America, he just vowed victory over the lethal terrorism, preparing its people for the prolonged war against terrorism. He said reportedly that he would lead the world to victory, now that war had been declared on his country and people."

"But, he has been blamed for his unilateral policy in the war with Saddam, even without getting approved by the

UN, and help from the allies such as France and Germany. What do you think about that?" I asked.

"I don't think President Bush is a unilateralist, but a cowboy-like conservative like his model, President Reagan. Mr. Reagan once called the Soviet Union 'the empire of evils'; and many people blamed him for his military build-up, calling him a warmonger. However, he became a final victor in the cold war, and kept the world from the possible nuclear war. In addition, Mr. Reagan gave us a stark lesson that we must prepare for war if we want to live in peace. Likewise, President Bush called the three countries of Iraq, Iran, and North Korea the 'axis of evils' openly. Well, his father had waged Gulf War I more than ten years ago, and Mr. Bush launched Gulf War II, on March 21, 2003. It seems like he has relied on his military forces almost one-sidedly in the prolonged war with terrorism, especially in Iraqi war named the 'Shock and Awe', following the ancient Chinese tactical strategy, 'Sunz tactics'. Well, the essence of the Sunz tactics is in the psychological warfare instead of actual fighting. As the Sunz tactical strategy is based on the Chinese natural philosophy, or Lao-tze's thought of Taoism of flowing water, which accomplishes much with no artificiality, following the natural providence ('wu-wei'), this ancient tactics puts first stress upon the victory with no or little fighting, the economical concept of warfare, I can say. We can quote many of his spiritual disciples in both West and East alike such as Napoleon, Rommel, Kong-ming, and Mao, Tse-tung.

"'Attack the mind of enemy!' is the first teaching of Sunz. In his tactics, the first strategy to take is to give a hard blow to enemy's fighting spirit and plan, then destroy its diplomatic relations or tear apart its allied forces, and third, the final worst, the actual fighting with enemies stationed in a castle. His tactical strategy can be said to be an economical one; and he warns us even the hurtfulness of victory in war that 'even the five series of victories can endanger the security of a nation', thus stressing upon the harmfulness of actual fighting. And in that sense, I don't think Napoleon got it fully the deep-hidden meaning of his spiritual master's strategy, the Sunz tactics."

"You mean, it is strongly demanded that President Bush use an engagement strategy in Iraq?" asked Mrs. Kim.

"The suicide bombers assaults of 9/11 robbed the US of its usual complacency; this giant super-power has now stood united, watching every foreigner with a strained and suspicious look as would-be a possible terrorist. Moreover, up to the unexampled test, Mr. Bush seems to have undertaken military action alone; and it can hardly stop the Islamic rage, but only to stir up the whole Moslems on the globe. In addition, as in the Sunz tactics, President Bush should launch a psychological war, trying to win the hearts and minds of the general Islamic people. In the far-off past in China, Hsiang Yu, a hero of Herculean strength and overwhelming spirit, had to kill himself, along with his beloved woman who plunged into a river, in his final battle with a libertine who tried to gain the confidence of the people. In the Orient, there goes the saying that 'The people's voice is the voice of God (Heaven)' like 'Vox populi, vox Dei'. I believe the major reason American GIs had to fight against heavy odds in Iraq after his official termination of warfare seems to be in the fact that he waged a military action alone, almost caring little about the Islamic culture, tradition, and sentiments, which seems to inflame Muslims negatively, I'm afraid."

"Mr. A used to say in his life-time that if a person wants to rid himself of bad karmas in his previous life, he should first repent of his former sins. Then, a person must keep on doing good deeds to others, and finally, pray to God for his country and world peace sincerely in every day life." I stopped awhile and continued.

"I think Americans should be wise enough to make 9/11 attacks the turning point of its history in the real sense of the word. As the US is one of the countries with the heaviest burden of bad karmas from the past, the white people should feel penitent in the minds about the evils and misdoings committed by their ancestors toward the native Indians and the black people in the bygone days.

Moreover, the WASPs should help, and do every kind of good deed to other people, especially to the Indian tribes and black people for their ancestors. In addition, as America is a country of Christianity, every white man is to lead a daily life with the Christian love for the people in need worldwide, especially those poverty-stricken people in Africa. That is why love is the best way to unburden ourselves of the baggage of bad karmas, along with suffering in life. Besides, the Christian people are to repent of ill doings their ancestors committed towards the Islamic people during the crusade expeditions in the middle age.

"Well, it may be said that now America has arrived at the turning point in its history. They should realize that 9/11 terror could form a dividing range to shed the burden of piled karmas from their shoulders, which may enable them to gain the spiritual rise for the bright future of their country, off from the possible nightmare of coming evils. Through their spiritual or moral rise, the American cowboy is to be able to 'lead and rule' the world nations, not as a trigger-happy cowboy (gunman) but as generous 'uncle' Sam."

CHAPTER 11
Epilogue: Over the Rainy Waves

In my college days, I liked English romantic poets; of romantic poets, I loved William Wordsworth, P.B. Shelley, and Lord Byron greatly. In 1980s, I say, I became a naturalist, kind of romanticist in a sense. I was wholly devoted to the Chinese natural philosophy, more specifically, the thought of Lao-tze, who had regarded the flowing water as the sole entity of Te (virtue), performing the heavenly Tao (way) on earth, and began to teach romantic poetry to university students.

Wordsworth lived a simple life surrounded by the natural beauty with high thinking in mind; and he thought that a poet could be a person speaking to people about 'how to live' in this prison-like world with his high sensibility of poetry. He loved nature deeply as a poet of nature, looking upon nature as the resting place of human being, feeling sick and tired of life in a city. He was a poet of nature as well as the poet of humanity, groping for the warm-hearted humanity in the bosom of nature.

Lord Byron was a passionate poet of genius, becoming an object of envy among all his fellow people at the age of 24. He viewed the history of humankind with the perspective based on the natural intimacy. He was the poet who was ready to sacrifice even his life for the sake of freedom of the Greek people. This handsome-looking romanticist, I think, lived along his short life with the dynamic spirit of blue waves ('Chongpa' in Korean) in his "The Ocean," churning wildly about the seashore.

P.B. Shelley was an eternal idealist, who revolted against all kinds of social injustice and political oppression in his lifetime. He longed for the pure-hearted love, freedom and justice even for the risk of his life. When I read his "Ode to the West Wind" aloud in the class, I always feel my heart beating, and I moved students by the powerful message of 'West Wind', the very image of young poet's undying ideal. He seems to have believed in the Oriental thought of transmigration or cycling rebirth as it is, just as a dead-looking tree in winter revives again in the forthcoming spring. Likewise, his frustrated thought and ideal, he firmly believed, would be sure to come alive in the days to come.

Late in the last year, I happened to talk with a nun in her small temple squatted at the foot of Mt. K, near my hometown. The middle-aged nun said, "Please feel free to go visit the nearby sea in your spare time; and naturally you'll get lots of unseen heavenly 'Ki (force)' from there; and it'll do you good for your health and life as well."

Almost everyone goes visit the sea in the summer, but seldom does in the cold winter. My wife and I, however, feel like seeing the winter sea, on and off. The deserted scene of the chilly winter sea looks lonesome and desolate in a degree, but gives a somewhat speculative mood and atmosphere, making us human beings absorbed in a thoughtful contemplation on life and even ourselves.

As my wife and I are poets on the literary stage within the country, we two like to travel together in and outside the country, when we can spare time and money.

During the last winter holidays, we went to see the blue waves in the winter sea on the Korean western coast. The blue waves were churning wildly along the seashore as usual, as if they would represent the image of eternity as well as the inner life-journey in this weary world.

There spread out a vast mud flat before our eyes. As before, the winter sea looked somewhat deserted; but some girls were strolling along on the tideland leisurely.

From the morning, it was raining all day long. The rain was beating on the face of seawater silently. On every side, from upward to down there, there was flowing water... from the clouded sky, on the wet tideland, and in the sea, where the waves were throwing up white clouds of spray on the rocks around the seashore off and on.

Some men were driving their cars along the wet mud flat, hardened almost like adobe by seawater for long; the cars were raising spray of water along their routes.

My wife was also driving her small car along the watery

tideland, tossing up white spray of seawater all the way.

Over the rainy sea waves, there were floating sea gulls wildly. The countless number of sea gulls flew back and forth in the rainy sky. They looked as if they would be mortals, roving over the rough sea of life, not knowing where to go.

The End

The Rise of An American Cowboy

by
Myung Un Lee

Available at your local bookstore or use this page to order.
-- 1-934020-31-1 - Lee, Myung Un   -

"PLEASE CALL FOR THE PRICE OF THIS BOOK"
Toll Free # 703-684-6895

Send to: New World Media Inc.
801 N. Pitt Street #123
Alexandria, VA 22314

Please send me the item above. I am enclosing
$________________(please add $4.50 per book to cover postage
and handling).

Send check, money order, or credit card:

Card #_________________________ Exp. date _____________

Mr./Mrs./Ms.____
Address____
City/State__________________________Zip________________

Please allow four to six weeks for delivery.
Prices and availability subject to change without notice.

Printed in the United States
112519LV00004B/7/A